Jane Austen
IN 50 PLACES AND OBJECTS

PAUL KENDALL

AMBERLEY

First published 2025

Amberley Publishing
The Hill, Stroud
Gloucestershire, GL5 4EP

www.amberley-books.com

ISBN 978 1 3981 2746 3 (print)
ISBN 978 1 3981 2747 0 (ebook)

British Library Cataloguing in Publication Data.
A catalogue record for this book is available from the British Library.

Typeset in 10pt on 13pt Celeste.
Typesetting by SJmagic DESIGN SERVICES, India.
Printed in the UK.

Appointed GPSR EU Representative:
Easy Access System Europe Oü, 16879218
Address: Mustamäe tee 50, 10621, Tallinn, Estonia
Contact Details: gpsr.requests@easproject.com, +358 40 500 3575

Contents

Acknowledgements

Among those who have helped me with this book are Lizzie Dunford at the Jane Austen House Museum, the Reverend Tim Bell and the PCC of St Nicholas, Steventon, and I am grateful for their kind permission to use images that I took at these places in this book. I thank Hampshire Cultural Trust for allowing me to use the images I took at Winchester City Museum. I thank Ewa Tylska for allowing me access to the Mercure Southampton Centre Dolphin Hotel to view the ballroom which was frequented by Jane Austen. I thank the staff of Chawton House for their permission to take photos during my visit. I extend my gratitude to the Dean and Chapter of Westminster for providing me with an image of Jane Austen's memorial in Westminster Abbey. I also thank the British Library Archive for providing the image of Jane Austen's portable writing desk. For her continued support, I thank my partner, Tricia Newsome.

Introduction

Jane Austen was the author of six novels, *Sense and Sensibility, Pride and Prejudice, Mansfield Park, Emma, Northanger Abbey* and *Persuasion,* the first four of these novels being published anonymously during her lifetime. It was not until after her death that Jane Austen was publicly acknowledged as the author of these books when her brother Henry included a biographical note in the publication of *Northanger Abbey* and *Persuasion.* Despite being an unknown author when she died, Austen left a remarkable legacy when her novels were finally recognised and became popular after her death.

The novels revolve around family, friendships, home life and love. They depict a quintessential view of middle-class domestic life in Regency Britian, through wit, irony and romantic themes. Austen had an ability to depict human emotions and gave an insight into contemporary manners. Money was important to survive in the world she inhabited, especially for the daughter of a Hampshire clergyman of limited means. There was immense pressure upon women in Jane's social circle to find a suitable husband and aspire to a contented home life. Jane Austen's female protagonists were no different. Jane tells the stories of the trials and tribulations of courtship which they endured as they set about trying to achieve the ultimate goal of security, marriage and a home to settle in, as well as fulfilment and happiness. Those women were like Jane, financially insecure and sometimes on the brink of penury. If Jane Austen had not belonged to a close-knit family, the members of which cared for each other, and if she had not had loving brothers, Jane may have become destitute. Austen highlighted the problems that women like herself had to confront with regards to gender inequality and the obstructions that had to be overcome in order to survive. Through her characters Elinor Dashwood, Elizabeth Bennet, Emma Woodhouse, Fanny Price, Catherine Morland and Anne Elliot we follow women of the time on their journeys though courtship to eventual marriage.

The social environment of her books excluded the aristocracy, the working classes and the impoverished and instead focused on the world that Jane was familiar with. As a member of the middle class, Jane Austen reflected her own social circle and presented a portrait of Regency society, culture and etiquette.

Despite having four novels published during her lifetime and receiving the admiration of the Prince Regent, the future King George IV, Jane was not widely famous. She would achieve prominence and recognition for the mass appeal of her work after her death. Her nephew James Austen-Leigh, who was also the youngest mourner at her funeral, wrote that 'even her fame may be said to be posthumous: it did not attain to any vigorous life till she had ceased to exist'.

Two-hundred years after she wrote her books, Austen continues to enamour her readers, having become a global phenomenon and selling millions of copies of books internationally alongside countless film and TV drama adaptations. Her appeal brings people together and Jane Austen societies have been established in the UK, North America and Australia. This book transports the reader to Regency Britain through places and objects associated with Jane Austen, presented in chronological order, and celebrates the brief life and inspirations of one of England's most celebrated authors.

Paul Kendall
July 2024

Author's Note

Geographical and digital map co-ordinates of the places and objects are provided for the reader to enter into Google maps on a mobile phone when visiting Jane Austen-related sites.

With the exception of Jane Austen's House, Chawton, where visitors are invited to look inside, most of the other buildings associated with Jane Austen featured in this book are privately owned. They can only be viewed from the road or footpath in a public space and are not to be approached.

1. Site of Steventon Rectory, Hampshire

Jane Austen's birthplace

Location: Junction of Steventon Road and the lane leading south to St Nicholas Church

Map co-ordinates: 51°13′41.1″N 1°12′50.0″W; decimal: 51.228072, -1.213881

On 16 December 1775, Jane Austen was born at Steventon Rectory, located in the corner of the field skirted by Steventon Road and the lane leading south to St Nicholas Church. All that remains of the rectory is a well with a pump which supplied water to the wash house at the rear of the rectory and is now concealed by a clump of undergrowth. The massive lime tree nearest the junction was planted by Jane's brother, James, during her lifetime and the existing hedgerows were a prominent feature when she lived here. Jane lived at Steventon Rectory for twenty-five years until 1801, which was most of her short life.

Jane was the seventh of eight children born to the Reverend George Austen and Cassandra Leigh. George wrote on the day following Jane's birth, 'Last night the time came, and without a great deal of warning, everything was soon happily over. We have now another girl, a present plaything for her sister Cassy, and a future companion.'

At Steventon Rectory, Jane would help with the daily chores and pursue her pastimes of reading and writing. Jane shared a dressing room with her sister Cassandra on the first floor of the rectory. It was here that Jane wrote *Love and Friendship* and *The History of England*, together with the initial drafts of her well-known novels *Sense and Sensibility*,

Steventon Rectory, the birthplace of Jane Austen, was situated in this field, looking south-east from Steventon Road to the road leading to St Nicholas Church. The undergrowth in the centre of the image conceals the well where the Austen family sourced water. The tall lime tree to the left was planted by James Austen, Jane's brother, during her lifetime. (Author's collection)

Pride and Prejudice and *Northanger Abbey*, although these were eventually published later during her life. According to her nephew James Austen-Leigh, who visited Steventon when he was a child, the dressing room that they shared led to a smaller chamber and this was where Jane's piano was situated. Jane learned how to play the piano during her childhood and was taught by George Chard, organist at Winchester Cathedral, who rode to Steventon Rectory to give her lessons.

Built in a valley, the rectory stands in a field with a grassy slope at the southern end of it. Jane Austen may have been inspired by her own childhood experiences when in *Northanger Abbey* she describes the protagonist Catherine Morland as a child who 'loved nothing so well in the world as rolling down the green slope at the back of the house'. As a young girl, Jane may have rolled down the grassy slope behind Steventon Rectory.

Left: Jane Austen's association with Steventon is acknowledged on signposts at the entrance to the village that bear a silhouette of her and proudly state 'Birthplace of Jane Austen, Steventon.' (Author's collection)

Below: Steventon Rectory, the birthplace of Jane Austen, which was demolished in 1824. (Author's collection)

2. St Nicholas Church, Steventon, Hampshire

Jane Austen's parish church

Location: St Nicholas Church, Steventon, RG25 3BE

Map co-ordinates: 51°13′17.2″N 1°12′46.3″W; decimal: 51.221444, -1.212872

St Nicholas Church was built during the twelfth century and the Reverend George Austen served as the rector of Steventon from 1761 until he retired, aged seventy, in 1801. Steventon was home to 300 parishioners and from the pulpit in St Nicholas Church Reverend Austen would have delivered his sermons to them, with Jane and the rest of the family sitting in the pews. The church stands as Jane would have known it except that a spire did not exist when she was a parishioner. The original steeple collapsed during a storm before George arrived and it was not replaced until the mid-nineteenth century.

Jane Austen worshipped in this church for over two decades. Her brother Henry wrote that 'she was thoroughly religious and devout; fearful of giving offence to God, and incapable of feeling it towards any fellow creature. On serious subjects she was well-instructed, both by reading and meditation, and her opinions accorded strictly with those of our Established Church.'

The Austen family would have regularly walked along the lane from the rectory to the church and perhaps the scenery has changed little since those days.

St Nicholas Church, Steventon. (Author's collection)

As an adolescent Jane mischievously filled out one of the specimen sheets at the front of one of the marriage registers of St Nicholas Church, using fictitious names. For the banns of marriage, she wrote, 'Henry Frederick Howard Fitzwilliam of London and Jane Austen of Steventon'. In the marriage entry that followed the banns, she named the groom as 'Arthur William Mortimer of Liverpool' with Jane as his bride. In the final statement, the groom is named as 'Jack Smith' and the bride is named 'Jane Smith, late Austen'. These imaginary husbands may have been one of Jane's first works of fiction. It is worth noting that Fitzwilliam was the Christian name of Mr Darcy in *Pride and Prejudice* and Jane made this entry in the marriage register years before she wrote the novel. Jane and her sister Cassandra were listed in the marriage register as attending the wedding of their cousin Jane Cooper to Captain Thomas Williams during December 1792 when they acted as witnesses to the nuptials.

The interior of St Nicholas Church, viewed from the pulpit where the Reverend George Austen delivered his sermons. Jane Austen would have sat in the pews in front of the pulpit. (Author's collection)

Halfway along the nave there is a bronze plaque dedicated to Jane Austen. It was unveiled in 1936 by Emma Austen-Leigh, the great-granddaughter of James Austen, Jane's brother. (Author's collection)

3. Reading Abbey Gateway, Berkshire

Jane Austen's school

Location: Abbot's Walk, Reading, RG1 3BD

Map co-ordinates: 51°27′23.4″N 0°58′00.6″W; decimal: 51.456505, -0.966819

During 1785, Jane and Cassandra were sent to Abbey House School, Reading, where they joined their cousin Jane Cooper. The establishment was run by Mrs Latournelle, an English woman named Sarah Hackitt who had married a Frenchman called Francis Latournelle. Mrs Latournelle had a cork leg and could not speak a word of French. She had to employ teachers to provide tuition for the girls. Mrs Sherwood, a former pupil who attended the school in 1790, wrote of the school, 'or rather the abbey itself, was exceedingly interesting ... the ancient building, which consisted of a gateway with rooms above, and on each side of it a vast staircase, of which the balustrades had originally been gilt'.

The Reverend George Austen paid extra for his daughters to become parlour boarders, which gave them the privilege of eating their daily meals with Mrs Latournelle in her parlour. The atmosphere and discipline at the school was relaxed and lessons for the pupils consisted of two hours in the morning, including needlework, grammar and French. The pupils had the freedom to do what they wanted for the remainder of the day. When their brothers Edward Austen and Edward Cooper visited them, the girls were permitted to accompany them to a local tavern near the school.

Jane Austen may have used her short time at the Abbey House School as inspiration when describing Mrs Goddard's school in her novel *Emma*, 'where girls might be sent to be out of the way and scramble themselves into a little education, without any danger of coming back prodigies'.

Educating Jane and Cassandra stretched the Austen finances and during 1786 they ceased to be parlour boarders and ate and lived in the dormitories with the other girls. The cost of his daughters' education eventually became unaffordable for the Reverend Austen, his payments to Mrs Latournelle having fallen into arrears by December 1786 when the girls returned home to Steventon.

Jane Austen was educated at Abbey House School which occupied Reading Abbey Gateway during 1785–86. (Author's collection)

4. Jane Austen's Portable Writing Desk

Jane Austen wrote her novels at this desk

Location: British Library, 96 Euston Road, London, NW1 2DB

Map co-ordinates: 51°31′43.5″N 0°07′38.1″W; decimal: 51.528758, -0.127235

Recognising that his daughter possessed a talent for writing, during December 1794, the Reverend George Austen purchased a portable mahogany writing desk from John Ring, who specialised in cabinet-making and upholstery in Basingstoke. The desk was likely a gift for Jane's nineteenth birthday. It is a tangible example of her father's encouragement of his daughter's writing abilities.

A year after receiving this desk, in 1795, Jane wrote *Elinor and Marianne,* later revised and renamed *Sense and Sensibility,* eventually published in October 1811. During October 1796, Jane began writing *First Impressions* (later renamed *Pride and Prejudice*), completing

Jane Austen's portable mahogany writing desk. In 2009, Joan Austen-Leigh presented the writing desk to the British Library so it could be preserved and displayed as an object of significant historic importance. It can be viewed in the Sir John Ritblat Gallery where it is a permanent exhibit as one of the Treasures of the British Library in London. (From the British Library Archive)

it within ten months by August 1797. It was written on this mahogany desk. After reading it to her family, during November 1797, Jane's father sent a letter to London publishers Cadell and Davies in an effort to get his daughter's work published. However, the proposal was rejected and the literary world would have to wait until January 1813 before it was published.

The writing desk was Jane's personal space and was always to hand, both at home and when she travelled. Once unlocked, the desk would open to form a sloped surface on which she could write her manuscripts and beneath that space was a compartment in which her manuscripts could be stored. The writing desk certainly accompanied her when she visited her brother in Kent and Jane was distressed when she nearly lost it during October 1798 after stopping off at the Bull and George Inn, Dartford. Soon after she arrived, her possessions were mistakenly placed on a post-chaise that was heading for Gravesend and then on to the West Indies, but fortunately the desk was recovered.

During 1798, Jane began writing *Susan*, which was renamed *Catherine* and would later evolve into *Northanger Abbey*, which was published posthumously. Jane wrote all her novels on this desk and her nephew James Edward Austen-Leigh referred to it in his memoir, confirming that *Emma*, *Mansfield Park* and *Persuasion* were certainly scribed on this desk while Jane was living at Chawton: 'In that well occupied female party, there must have been many precious hours of silence during which the pen was busy at the little mahogany writing desk, while Fanny Price, or Emma Woodhouse, or Anne Elliot was growing into beauty and interest.'

The business premises of John Ring, who made Jane's writing desk, were in this building at No. 81 Church Street, Basingstoke. (Author's collection)

5. The Red House, Sevenoaks, Kent

Jane Austen's first visit to the county known as the 'Garden of England'

Location: 50 High Street, Sevenoaks, Kent, TN13 1JL

Map co-ordinates: 51°16′09.1″N 0°11′36.4″E; decimal: 51.269203, 0.193438

Francis Austen was uncle to the Reverend George Austen and great-uncle to Jane. George's family originated in Kent and Francis established a legal practice in Sevenoaks, where he purchased Red House during 1743. Constructed in 1686 by Thomas Couchman, Red House is occupied by a legal firm today.

When George Austen was orphaned Francis Austen cared for him and paid for his education at Tonbridge School and St John's College, Oxford. Francis also secured the parish of Deane as a living for George in addition to Steventon, which had been granted to him by Thomas Knight. The Reverend George Austen appreciated the support that his uncle had provided and kept in close contact with him. During summer 1788, George and his wife visited his family living in west Kent. Jane, who was aged twelve, and Cassandra, who was aged fifteen, accompanied their parents. This was Jane Austen's first recorded visit to Kent. Francis, who was aged ninety, invited them to dinner at Red House on 22 July 1788. Philadelphia Walter, known as Philly, the niece of George Austen, also attended that dinner and met her cousins Jane and Cassandra for the first time. In a letter to her brother James, Philly reputedly provided the first written description of Jane and her family:

The Red House, where Jane Austen visited her great-uncle. (Author's collection)

> Yesterday I began an acquaintance with my two female cousins, Austen's. My uncle, aunt, Cassandra and Jane arrived at Mr. F. Austen's the day before ... The youngest [Jane] is very like her brother Henry, not at all pretty and very prim, unlike a girl of twelve; but it is hasty judgement which you will scold me.

Philly respected Cassandra but continued to be critical of Jane and in another letter, written two days later, she wrote, 'the more I see of Cassandra the more I admire [her]. Jane is whimsical and affected.' It must be borne in mind that Philly was fourteen years older than Jane, who was not yet a teenager, while Cassandra was fifteen and could probably relate more to their elder cousin.

Three years after Jane Austen stayed at Red House, Sevenoaks, her great-uncle Francis Austen died there at the age of ninety-two on 21 June 1791.

6. Ashe Rectory, Ashe, Hampshire

Jane Austen developed a relationship with her neighbour Anne Lefroy here

Location: Ashe Lane, Ashe, RG25 3AQ (private property)

Map co-ordinates: 51°14′42.5″N 1°14′07.6″W; decimal: 51.245146, -1.235451

The Reverend George Lefroy and his wife Anne moved into Ashe Rectory in 1783 and became friends of the Austen family, who were their nearest neighbours. Sir Egerton Brydges, the brother of Anne Lefroy, recalled ,'I remember Jane Austen, the novelist, a little child: she was very intimate with Mrs Lefroy, and much encouraged by her.'

Jane would regularly visit Anne Lefroy, who was twenty-six years her senior, at Ashe Rectory. The two women shared a passion for literature and Anne allowed Jane use of their library. Anne Lefroy hosted dances within Ashe Rectory, where she created a dancing space by opening the dividing doors between the morning room and the dining room. People living in rural communities had to create their own entertainment and there were several large houses close to Steventon Rectory which held regular dances that Jane and the Austens were invited to. These were communal affairs with attendees familiar with each other. It is possible that the ball that Jane described in a letter of 24 December 1798 may have taken place at Ashe Rectory as she mentions that Mrs Lefroy admired the black cap that she was wearing. Of the ball, Jane wrote:

> Our ball was very thin, but by no means unpleasant. There were thirty-one people, and only eleven ladies out of the number, and by five single women in the room ... There were twenty dances and I danced them all, and without any fatigue. I was glad to find myself capable of

Ashe Rectory. (Author's collection)

> dancing so much, and with so much satisfaction as I did; from my slender enjoyment of the Ashford balls (as assemblies for dancing) I had not thought myself equal to it, but in cold weather and with few couples I fancy I could just as well dance for a week together as for half an hour.

It was during a visit to Ashe Rectory around December 1795 that Jane met Anne's Irish nephew Tom Lefroy. He was a law student studying in London and was spending Christmas with his uncle and aunt at Ashe Rectory. Jane and Tom were attracted to each other, but Tom had to continue his studies in London. Anne Lefroy may have felt sorry that the friendship between Jane and her nephew did not blossom into a lasting relationship. Anne Lefroy invited the Reverend Samuel Blackall to stay at Ashe Rectory during 1797, introducing him to Jane in the hope that they would be a suitable match. However, this faltered because he declined an invite to return to the rectory during the following year.

Anne Lefroy died after falling from her horse on Jane's twenty-ninth birthday on 16 December 1804.

7. All Saints' Church and Deane House, Deane, Hampshire

Jane Austen visited her friends, the Lloyd family

Location: Manor Farm Lane, Deane (to access the church, use the public footpath which passes through the garden of Deane House, a private property; please stay on the public footpath – the house can be seen looking north from this path)

Map co-ordinates: 51°14′53.2″N 1°13′03.6″W; decimal: 51.248122, -1.217677

Before Jane was born, the Reverend George Austen was once rector of the parish of Deane and conducted services in the church which once stood within the estate of Deane House. The church that would have been familiar to Jane was demolished in 1818. The current All Saints' Church was built in 1820. George Austen lived with his wife Cassandra at Deane Rectory after their wedding from 1764 and remained there until July 1768, when Steventon Rectory was being refurbished to make it habitable to live in. It was at Deane Rectory that Jane's three elder brothers, James, George and Edward, were born. James was born on 13 February 1765, George, on 26 August 1766 and Edward on 7 October 1767. During 1789, the Reverend George Austen leased Deane Rectory to Mrs Lloyd, the widow of a fellow rector, and she moved in with her two daughters, Mary and Martha Lloyd, who would become friends with the Austens and later marry two of Jane's brothers. Jane would frequently walk to Deane Rectory from Steventon to visit Mary and Martha.

Deane House was built in 1786 close to All Saints' Church and was the home of the Harwood family for several generations. Many social events were held in the house and Jane Austen was invited to various balls there during her lifetime. It was here that she

All Saints' Church, Deane, Hampshire. (Author's collection)

Deane House, Deane, Hampshire. (Author's collection)

danced with Tom Lefroy on 9 January 1796. Jane attended another ball at Deane House during October 1800, but none of the male guests made an impression upon her. In a letter to Cassandra on 1 November 1800, she wrote:

> I dined and slept at Deane ... It was a pleasant ball, and still more good than pleasant, for there were nearly sixty people, and sometimes we had seventeen couples. The Portsmouths, Dorchesters, Boltons, Portals, and Clerks were there, and all the meaner and more usual &c., &c.'s. There was a scarcity of men in general, and a still greater scarcity of any that were good for much. I danced nine dances out of ten – five with Stephen Terry, T. Chute, and James Digweed, and four with Catherine [Bigg]. There was commonly a couple of ladies standing up together, but not often any so amiable as ourselves.

While attending social functions such as the dances held at Deane House Jane took note of people, their mannerisms and behaviours, and incorporated them in her novels.

8. Assembly Room Plaque, Basingstoke, Hampshire

Jane Austen attended dances here

Location: 3 Winchester Street, Basingstoke, RG21 7QA

Map co-ordinates: 51°15′44.8″N 1°05′14.0″W; decimal: 51.262448, -1.087220

A plaque marks the site of the Assembly Rooms where Jane Austen attended balls while she lived in Steventon up to 1801. The ballroom was a hayloft above the stables at the rear of the Angel Inn, a coaching station. During the winter, dances were held each month in towns such as Basingstoke. They were attended by affluent families from the local neighbourhood. Two lines of ladies and gentlemen would engage in country dances within this space. Jane Austen regularly attended these balls, her elder brother Henry writing that 'she was fond of dancing and excelled in it'.

Going to an assembly or a ball was an opportunity to wear fine clothes and for young ladies and gentlemen to meet, albeit in a restrictive environment. They would be watched and there existed a strict protocol to adhere to while engaging with members of the opposite sex, whether at dinner parties or dances. To protect the reputation of a young lady, a woman would not display haste in responding to the attentions of a young gentleman until that man's intentions were revealed. This etiquette safeguarded the woman from misreading the situation, reduced the risk of disappointment and prevented her from being embarrassed in front of family and friends.

On the dance floor, a couple would be forbidden to address each other by their Christian names unless they were family friends. Physical touching was not allowed except the brief holding of a hand during a dance. Sharing a coach and exchanging gifts and letters were also frowned upon. If any of these actions were seen to have taken place, then the couple would be regarded as engaged.

A plaque commemorating the site of the Basingstoke Assembly Room, where Jane Austen attended dances. (Author's collection)

The statue of Jane Austen in Church Street, Basingstoke, situated outside the Willis Museum and opposite the plaque marking the site of the Assembly Rooms where Jane regularly danced. Basingstoke is 7 miles north-east of Steventon and was the closest town to Jane's home. As well as attending assemblies there, she visited the town for shopping. The statue depicts her during her frequent visits to the town when she may have been shopping or, given that she is clutching a book, visiting a library or bookshop. (Author's collection)

Jane Austen liked dancing, and balls were featured in the plots of her novel as pastimes enjoyed by the principal characters. It is reputed that she may have attended balls in Basingstoke during her later teen years from 1791 until 1794. Jane wrote in a letter dated 17 November 1798, 'There is to be a ball at Basingstoke next Thursday. Our assemblies have very kindly declined ever since we laid down the carriage, so that dis-inclination to go have kept pace together.'

By the time Jane Austen moved to Bath she had lost interest in the dances held in Basingstoke for she lamented that 'the Basingstoke balls are certainly on the decline'. As she grew older, Jane may have become tired of the same venue and the same faces attending the dances which restricted the chance of meeting a potential husband. She may have been yearning for different horizons, places and dance partners.

9. Deane Gate Inn Coaching Station, Deane, Hampshire

The Austen family caught coaches from here

Location: The Palm Brasserie, Andover Road, Deane, RG25 3AX

Map co-ordinates: 51°14′44.8″N 1°13′00.9″W; decimal: 51.245788, -1.216917

Situated a mile-and-a-quarter north of Steventon, this building was once a coaching station known as the Deane Gate Inn. It was here that the Austen family boarded horse-drawn coaches bound for Basingstoke and London.

The only means of travelling vast distances in England during Jane Austen's lifetime was on horseback or using horse-drawn carriages. The Austen women would have travelled by post-chaise, a more costly method requiring changes of horses at inns but providing greater comfort and privacy.

Deane Gate Inn was the starting point for Jane's numerous journeys to Kent to visit her brother Edward. It was a 60-mile journey from the coaching house at Deane to the White Horse Cellars Coaching Inn in Piccadilly, London, which would take seven to eight hours before continuing the journey to Godmersham Park, near Canterbury, Kent.

If a person wanted to travel by coach instead of post-chaise without booking in advance, there was no guarantee that they would be able to board. Jane's brother Charles attempted to catch a coach, Jane writing on 21 January 1799 that, 'he attempted to go to town last night, and got as far on his road thither as Deane Gate, but both coaches were full, and we had the pleasure of seeing him back again'.

The Palm Brasserie at Deane was once Deane Gate Inn coaching station, which was used by the Austen family. (Author's collection)

10. Godmersham Park, Kent

Jane Austen's brother Edward inherited the estate in 1798
Location: ABDO College (no public access)
Map co-ordinates: private property; decimal: private property

Built in 1732 and situated in the Stour Valley between Ashford and Canterbury, Godmersham Park was the home of the Knight family. Jane's elder brother was fortunate to inherit this estate along with Steventon and Chawton in Hampshire. The Reverend George Austen was the second cousin of Jane Knight, and it was the Knight family who appointed him as rector of Steventon in 1764. In 1779, Jane's son Thomas married Catherine, and he took her on a tour of the family estates at Godmersham, Steventon and Chawton during their honeymoon. They called upon the Austens at Steventon Rectory where they were introduced to Edward, Jane Austen's brother, then aged thirteen. They were impressed with his good manners and decided to allow him to accompany them on their grand tour of Europe between 1786 and 1788. The Knights regularly invited Edward to stay with them during the summer months. As the Knights remained childless, they decided to make Edward heir to their estates in 1783. Childless couples would often foster or adopt a distant relative and raise them as their own child, even if both parents were still alive. George and Cassandra Austen saw this as an opportunity for a good start in life for one of their sons.

Thomas Knight died in 1794, and his wife, Catherine, inherited the estate. Catherine asked Edward to live in Godmersham Park and manage the estate during August 1798. Edward inherited Godmersham Park and the Steventon and Chawton estates when Catherine died in 1812; as a condition of the inheritance, he had to change his name to Knight. His descendants have owned Chawton House since then.

Jane Austen visited her brother at Godmersham Park in 1798. She became a regular visitor and developed a fondness for the county of Kent, writing, 'Kent is the only place for happiness; everybody is rich there.'

Living within the grandeur of a stately home such as Godmersham Park was an overwhelming experience for Jane. She stayed there from June to September 1808 and during that time Jane wrote to Cassandra, 'I am in the Yellow Room – very literally – for

Godmersham Park, Kent. (Alamy)

I am writing in at this moment. It seems odd to me to have such a great place all to myself, and to be at Godmersham.'

It is clear that sometimes Jane felt like the poor relation when staying at Godmersham Park. During her visit in August 1805, Mr Hall dressed the hair of Elizabeth Knight, her sister-in-law and lady of the house, charging 5*s*. However, he charged Jane a lot less. Writing to Cassandra, she observed:

> Towards me he was as considerate as I had hoped for from my relationship to you, charging me only 2s. 3d. for cutting my hair, though it was as thoroughly dressed after being cut for Eastwell as it had been for the Ashford assembly. He certainly respects either our youth or our poverty.

While at Godmersham Park, Jane entertained her nieces and nephews as well as going on shopping excursions to Canterbury. She continued to write her novels. Edward's daughter Marianne Knight recalled, 'Aunt Jane would sit very quietly at work beside the fire in Godmersham library, then suddenly burst out laughing, jump up, cross the room to a distant table with papers lying upon it, write something down, returning presently and sitting down quietly to her work again'.

Above: Godmersham Park and the surrounding estate. (Alamy)

Left: The entrance hall at Godmersham Park, Kent. (Alamy)

11. No. 13 Queen's Square, Bath

Jane Austen resided here during 1799

Location: 13 Queen's Square, Bath, BA1 2HH

Map co-ordinates: 51°22′58.8″N 2°21′49.8″W; decimal: 51.383005, -2.363839

Jane Austen visited Bath for the first time during November 1797, when she stayed with her uncle and aunt, James and Jane Leigh-Perrot. James was the only brother of Jane's mother Cassandra Leigh and after inheriting property at Northleigh, Oxfordshire, he adopted the name from his benefactor Perrot. Two years later, Jane Austen made a second trip to Bath. When her

The house at No. 13 Queen's Square, where Jane Austen lived for six weeks during 1799. (Author's collection)

brother Edward was suffering from gout during spring 1799, he decided to try the waters of Bath to alleviate the discomfort caused by this condition. Jane and her mother accompanied Edward and his family, a visit that lasted six weeks. They lived at No. 13 Queen's Square from 17 May to 26 June 1799. On the day of her arrival, Jane reported to Cassandra on 17 May:

> Well, here we are at Bath; we got here about one o'clock, and have arrived just long enough to go over the house, fix on our rooms, and be very well pleased with the whole of it ... We are exceedingly pleased with the house. The rooms are quite as large as we expected.

Jane and her mother stayed on the second floor, 'where we have two nice sized rooms, with dirty quilts and everything comfortable'.

Queen's Square was the first square built in Bath during the 1730s and was regarded as a stylish quarter of the city when Jane stayed there in 1799. However, sixteen years later, when Jane wrote *Persuasion,* it had become less fashionable. In the novel, Mrs Musgrove did not like this location and wrote rather disdainfully 'none of your Queen's Squares for us!'.

While in Bath, Edward drank at the Hetling Pump Room, bathed in the waters and received electricity treatment. The sojourn in Bath alleviated Edward's gout and he lived for another fifty-three years until December 1852 when he died aged eighty-five.

The house opposite No. 13 Queen's Square on the corner of Chapel Row and Princes Street was favoured by Mrs Austen when searching for a home in Bath in 1801. It was probably a matter of cost or unavailability which precluded the Austens from finding a suitable and affordable place in this location.

12. Sydney Gardens, Bath

Pleasure gardens enjoyed by Jane Austen

Location: Sydney Gardens, Bathwick, Bath, BA2 6NH

Map co-ordinates: 51°23′09.7″N 2°21′00.8″W; decimal: 51.386020, -2.350208

Sydney Gardens opened in 1795, allowing the people of Bath to enjoy the gardens, walk through a maze and play on the bowling greens. Construction of the Avon and Kennet Canal commenced in 1800, the canal dissecting the gardens with two cast-iron bridges built over it. Visitors had to pass through a hotel, was named Sydney House, to access Sydney Gardens. The Sydney Hotel, which faced west towards Great Pulteney Street, is now the Holburne Museum. It had a ballroom for dances and offered public breakfasts. When Jane stayed in Bath during May 1799, she mentioned that 'there is a public breakfast in Sydney Gardens every morning, so that we shall not be wholly starved'.

During the summer months, Sydney Gardens was a venue for music concerts and firework displays, which Jane Austen no doubt appreciated, writing:

> There is to be a grand gala on Tuesday evening in Sydney Gardens, a concert with illuminations and fireworks. To the latter Elizabeth [her niece] and I look forward with pleasure, and even the concert will have more than its usual charm for me, as the gardens are large enough for me to get pretty well beyond reach of its sound.

Sydney Gardens Hotel was once the entrance to Sydney Gardens. It is now known as the Holburne Museum. (Author's collection)

The rear of the Sydney Gardens Hotel, painted by John Claude Nattes, 1804. (Author's collection)

Each gala night attracted as many as 4,000 people with an entrance fee of 2*s* 6*d* per person. Jane returned to Sydney Gardens on 18 June 1799, writing:

> Last night we were in Sydney Gardens again, as there was a repetition of the gala which went off so ill on the 4th. we did not go till nine, and then were in good time for the fireworks, which were really beautiful, and surpassing my expectation; the illuminations too were very pretty.

Sydney Gardens is opposite No. 4 Sydney Place, where the Austens lived between 1801 and 1804, so Jane must have frequented these pleasure gardens regularly.

13. No. 1 Paragon, Bath

Jane Austen lived here while searching for a suitable residence in Bath

Location: No. 1 Paragon, Bath, BA1 5LX

Map co-ordinates: 51°23′09.7″N 2°21′36.8″W; decimal: 51.386020, -2.360234

This was the home of Jane Austen's affluent uncle and aunt, James and Jane Leigh-Perrot, which they leased during the winter season between 1797 until 1810. Mrs Austen took Jane and Cassandra to stay with the Leigh-Perrots at No. 1 Paragon during 1797. Jane is also recorded as visiting them at this address during 1799. Jane's visits to Bath would inspire her to write *Northanger Abbey* the following year.

When the Reverend George Austen suddenly announced his retirement in 1801 and decided to move to Bath with his wife and two daughters, the family had to find permanent accommodation. While Jane and her mother searched for a home they stayed with the Leigh-Perrots at No. 1 Paragon from 4 May 1801. Jane enjoyed staying in a room by herself and in a letter to Cassandra on 5 May 1801 she wrote: 'I have the pleasure of writing from my own room up two pair of stairs, with everything very comfortable about me.' However, Jane did not enjoy the tedious parties that her aunt hosted. On 12 May 1801, she reported to Cassandra, 'another stupid party last night; perhaps if larger they might be less intolerable, but here there were just enough to make one card-table, with six people to look on and talk nonsense to each other'.

Mrs Leigh-Perrot wanted the Austens to take the property adjacent to No. 1 Paragon, but Jane was not comfortable living so close to her aunt and wrote, 'Mrs Perrot will want to get us into Oxford Buildings, but we all unite in particular dislike of that part of the town, and therefore hope to escape.'

Right: Jane Austen stayed with her aunt at No. 1 Paragon, Bath, the building on the left in this image. (Author's collection)

Far right: The rear of No. 1 Paragon, which is the second house to the right of the stairs. (Author's collection)

14. No. 4 Sydney Place, Bath

Jane Austen lived here

Location: No. 4 Sidney Place, Bathwick, Bath, BA2 6NF

Map co-ordinates: 51°23′09.4″N 2°21′05.9″W; decimal: 51.385952, -2.351641

Jane Austen eventually found suitable, affordable accommodation for her family at No. 4 Sydney Place when she saw an advertisement in the *Bath Chronicle* on 21 May 1801 which stated:

> TO BE DISPOSED OF THE LEASE OF No. 4 SYDNEY PLACE, three years and a quarter of which are unexpired at midsummer. The situation is desirable, the rent very low and the landlord is bound by covenant to paint the two first floors this summer – A premium will therefore be expected.

Jane Austen's home at No. 4 Sydney Place. (Author's collection)

Sydney Place comprised recently built terraced houses at the eastern end of Pulteney Street, overlooking Sydney Gardens. Completed in 1792, the terrace was part of the development commissioned by Sir William Pulteney. Sydney Place was in the suburbs of Bath where the countryside meets the town. Although No. 4 Sydney Gardens was further from the centre of Bath, it was a sufficiently large house to accommodate Jane, her parents and her sister. The annual rent was £150, which her father could afford from his £600 annual pension, and the house was situated directly opposite Sydney Gardens, which pleased Jane. The Austens decided upon No. 4 Sydney Gardens as the place to live in Bath, taking possession of their new lodgings during October 1801.

No. 4 Sydney Place is a four-storey house with a cellar. There were two rooms on each floor, one facing Sydney Gardens while the other faced the garden. The dining room and Reverend Austen's study were on the ground floor. The Austens would spend most of the day on the first floor where the two drawing rooms could be converted into one large space by opening the interconnecting doors. Here they would receive visitors. There were three bedrooms on the third floor, one for her parents, probably at the front of the house, one for Jane and Cassandra to share, at the rear, and a guestroom. The three servants that worked for the Austens lived in the attic which formed the fourth floor.

Mrs Austen and Jane had decided that the Reverend Austen could afford three servants, even though he was not consulted about the decision. On 3 January 1801, prior to moving to Sydney Place, Jane wrote:

> My mother looks forward with as much certainty as you can do to our keeping two maids; my father is the only one not in the secret. We plan having a steady cook and a young, giddy housemaid, with a sedate middle-aged man, who is to undertake the double office of husband to the former and sweetheart to the latter.

The Austens could not afford the rent increase when the lease expired in September 1804 and they moved to cheaper accommodation at No. 3 Green Park Buildings.

A plaque commemorating Jane Austen's occupancy of No. 4 Sydney Place. It states that she lived here until 1805, which is factually incorrect as the Austens vacated the building in 1804. (Author's collection)

15. The Pump Room, Bath

A social setting that featured in Northanger Abbey *and* Persuasion

Location: Pump Room, Abbey Churchyard, Bath, BA1 1LZ

Map co-ordinates: 51°22′52.7″N 2°21′35.4″W; decimal: 51.381308, -2.359674

The Pump Room was originally built by John Harvey in 1706. The current building was constructed by Thomas Baldwin between 1793 and 1796. The Pump Room was the destination for Georgian society to be seen, to socialise, to promenade and posture, to discuss politics and to gossip but primarily to 'take the waters' from the hot springs. Pierce Egan wrote in 1819 that, 'The Great Pump Room is completely open for the reception of the public, no etiquette of rank being required to obtain an admission; and the only qualification necessary to join the gay throng, without ceremony, is that of a clean decent appearance.'

In her first letter written after moving to Bath, Jane mentions walking from No. 1 Paragon to the Pump Room and she refers to her uncle 'taking his second glass of water'.

Jane Austen frequented the Pump Room and mentioned it in her novels *Northanger Abbey* and *Persuasion*. In *Northanger Abbey*, Jane wrote that the morning routine for

Above: The Pump Room as depicted in Thomas Rowlandson's cartoon *Comforts of Bath*, 1798. (The Elisha Whittelsey Collection, The Elisha Whittelsey Fund, 1959, The Met Museum, New York)

Left: The entrance to the Grand Pump Room, Bath. (Author's collection)

Catherine Morland and Mrs Allen was to visit the shops and the Pump Room where 'they paraded up and down for an hour, looking at every body and speaking to no one'. On another occasion, Catherine and the Allens:

> Set off in good time for the Pump Room where the ordinary course of events and conversation took place: Mr Allen, after drinking his glass of water, joined some gentlemen to talk over the politics of the day and compare the accounts of their newspapers; and the ladies walked about together, noticing every new face, and almost every new bonnet in the room.

In *Northanger Abbey*, Catherine Morland meets Henry Tilney in the Pump Room and when she returned to search for him there the following day, she described the place as where:

> ... every creature in Bath, except himself, was to be seen in the room at different periods of the fashionable hours. Crowds of people were every moment passing in and out, up the steps and down; people whom nobody cared about, and nobody wanted to see; and he only was absent.

Catherine Morland was not enamoured with her experience in the Pump Room because of the people there who she described as 'unsupportable, and that there was not a genteel face to be seen'.

Most of the Georgian features of the Pump Room remain today, including the marble vase that pours rejuvenating spa water.

The Pump Room now serves as a restaurant. (Alamy)

16. Bath Assembly Rooms

Jane Austen attended dances here

Location: Bath Assembly Rooms, Bennett Street, Bath, BA1 2QH

Map co-ordinates: 51°23′10.2″N 2°21′46.5″W; decimal: 51.386157, -2.362929

Construction began on the Bath Assembly Rooms in 1769, and they opened in 1771. This venue became the epicentre of social life in Bath during the Georgian era, where music concerts and assemblies took place on alternate nights. Assemblies were evening events which included dancing, card playing, observing people, gossiping and drinking tea. Pierce Egan recorded that during 1816 there was a Dress Ball on Monday nights, concerts on Wednesday evenings, Fancy Ball on Thursday nights followed by a Card Assembly on Friday nights. The rooms were open every day except for the Card Room, which was closed on Sundays.

It was here that ladies enjoyed to dance, which provided both an opportunity to exercise and make friends. It was also a chance for ladies to wear their fine dresses and flirt with the opposite sex. Unlike the balls held in the provincial town halls, assemblies and those held at the homes of friends and neighbours in Steventon where everyone knew each other, the dances held in the Assembly Rooms in Bath were a public affair where dancing partners were introduced by the Master of the Ceremonies. In *Northanger Abbey*, Catherine Morland was introduced to Henry Tilney by Mr King, the Master of Ceremonies in the Lower Assembly Room, Bath.

The Assembly Rooms at Bath contained a Tea Room, an Octagon Room (which was also known as the Tea Room where cards were played), an Upper and Lower assembly room, each known as the Ballroom. Two Master of the Ceremonies presided over both assembly rooms. Only the Upper Assembly Room remains, the Lower Assembly Room having been destroyed in 1820.

The exterior of the Assembly Rooms, Bath. (Author's collection)

The Upper Assembly Room could accommodate between 800 and 1,200 people. A ball began around 6 p.m. The dancers stood in two lines opposite their partners and the synchronised movements of each of the partners in unison was a display of elegance which was enjoyable for both the participants and spectators, who observed from the side of the ballroom. A ball would start with a minuet which would be danced by two people, involving bows and courtesies with slow, sedate and graceful movements, forwards, backwards and sideways interspersed with complicated spins and twirls.

When the minuet was concluded, the lady would return to her seat and the Master of the Ceremonies would bring another lady to the gentleman for him to dance with. Minuets were danced for a two-hour period during which ladies and gentlemen were introduced. The country dances began at 8 p.m. and this time the ladies, according to social status, began the dances. At 9 p.m. there was a short interlude for tea and then the revelries continued until 11 p.m. when the music stopped. The cessation of music at 11 p.m. was a rule introduced by Beau Nash during his tenure as Master of the Ceremonies. There were certain rules that had to be complied with. The ladies had to wear lappets, a piece of lace that was attached to their headdress as a means of identification. Gentlemen had to change

The cartoonist Thomas Rowlandson captures a scene that Jane Austen would have been familiar with in *The Comforts of Bath*, in 1798. (The Elisha Whittelsey Collection, The Elisha Whittelsey Fund, 1959, The Met Museum, New York)

partners after two dances to ensure that each lady had the opportunity to dance. James Morland tried to violate this rule by seeking further dances with Isabella Thorpe without changing partners in *Northanger Abbey*. Isabella confided in Catherine Morland, 'He wants me to dance with him again, though I tell him that it is a most improper thing; and entirely against the rules. It would make us the talk of the place, if we were not to change partners.'

Jane Austen writes about attending her first ball at the Assembly Rooms soon after her arrival in Bath in a letter dated 12 May 1801. She was not enthralled by the experience in the Tea Room:

> I dressed myself as well as I could, and had all my finery much admired at home. By nine o'clock, my uncle, aunt, and I entered the rooms and linked Miss Winstone on to us. Before tea it was rather a dull affair; but then the before tea did not last long, for there was only one dance, danced by four couple. Think of four couple, surrounded by a hundred people, dancing in the Upper Rooms.
>
> After tea we cheered up; the breaking up of private parties sent some scores more to the ball, and though it was shockingly and inhumanly thin for this place, there were people enough, to have made five or six pretty Basingstoke assemblies.

Jane's personal experience in the Bath Assembly Rooms is relived in *Northanger Abbey* through the character of Catherine Morland when she attended a ball with Mrs Allen. In *Persuasion*, Anne Elliot hoped to find Captain Wentworth in the Assembly Rooms.

The Ballroom in the Assembly Rooms, Bath. (Roger Garfield/Alamy)

17. Pyne House, Lyme Regis, Dorset

Jane Austen's holiday lodging

Location: No. 10 Broad Street, Lyme Regis, DT7 3QD

Map co-ordinates: 50°43′28.6″N 2°56′01.9″W; decimal: 50.724599, -2.933850

While living in Bath, Jane Austen and her family visited Lyme Regis on the Dorset coastline on two occasions, in 1803 and 1804. On 5 November 1803, there was a fire in Mill Lane and the only evidence that suggests Jane was in Lyme Regis at that time was her reference to it in a letter five years later, dated 7 October, when she described that fire: 'The flames were considerable, they seemed about as near to us as those at Lyme, and to reach higher.'

Jane returned to Lyme, as it was referred to then, with her parents, her sister Cassandra and her brother Henry and his wife, Eliza, between September and November 1804, when

Above: Pyne House, Lyme Regis. (Author's collection)

Right: This plaque commemorates Jane Austen's assumed association with Pyne House. (Author's collection)

the weather was mild in this part of Britain. Another attraction of this resort was its affordability. John Feltham wrote in 1806:

> Lodgings and boarding at Lyme are not merely reasonable, they are even cheap; the dissipations for the healthy, and the suitable accommodations for the sick, are within reach of ordinary resources. It is frequented by persons in the middle class of life, who go there, not always in search of their lost health, but as frequently perhaps to heal their wounded fortunes, or to replenish their exhausted revenues.

The Austens are reputed to have lodged at No. 10 Broad Street, which was owned by landlord W. Pyne, for part of summer 1804, until Cassandra, Henry and Eliza went to Weymouth. The building is named Pyne House after its landlord and was close to the beach and the Assembly Rooms where regular dances were held. The rear of Pyne House overlooked the beach. In a letter written on 14 September 1804 Jane mentions a dispute with Mr Pyne over the cost of a damaged item in the cottage.

> I have written to Buller & I have written to Mr Pyne, on the subject of the broken lid; it was valued by Anning here we were told at five shillings, & as that appeared to us beyond the value of all the furniture in the room together, we have referred ourselves to the owner.

The Assembly Room, frequented by Jane Austen and where weekly balls took place, was located at the bottom of Broad Street within walking distance of Pyne House. It overlooked the beach, but is now a car park, adjacent to the Rock Point Inn, which was built around 1790 and would have been known to Jane Austen.

The Rock Point Inn, which was built around 1790. The Assembly Rooms were adjacent to the inn but have been replaced by a car park next to the beach at Lyme Regis. Jane Austen would have been familiar with this inn. (Author's collection)

18. Replica of King George III's Bathing Machine, Weymouth, Dorset

Jane Austen bathed in the sea at Lyme Regis

Location: 70 Esplanade, Weymouth, DT4 8DE

Map co-ordinates: 50°36′43.5″N 2°27′13.3″W; decimal: 50.612087, -2.453693

Jane Austen bathed in the sea at Lyme Regis and probably used a bathing machine similar to the replica of the one used by King George III which is displayed at Weymouth. His Majesty set a trend for bathing in the sea in Georgian Britain and he did so on many occasions during his numerous visits to Weymouth.

The bathing machine was a private space in which to change in and out of swimming clothes and could be pulled by men or horses into the sea from where the occupants would enter the water. Jane Austen certainly bathed in the sea at Lyme Regis and would have used a bathing machine. In her letter dated 14 September 1804 she wrote, 'I continue quite well; in proof of which I have bathed again this morning. It was absolutely necessary that I should have the little fever and indisposition which I had: it has been all the fashion this week in Lyme.'

Jane enjoyed bathing in the sea at Lyme Regis so much that on another occasion she spent too long in the water. She wrote:

> The bathing was so delightful this morning & Molly so pressing with me to enjoy myself that I believe I staid in rather too long, as since the middle of the day I have felt unreasonably tired. I shall be more careful another time, & shall not bathe tomorrow as intended.

A replica of King George III's bathing machine at Weymouth. (Author's collection)

Left: A statue of King George III overlooks the bathing machine. Although his reign spanned Austen's life, the period is called Regency because George, Prince of Wales ruled Britain as the Prince Regent when his father became incapacitated due to mental illness between 1811 until the king's death in 1820. (Author's collection)

Below: Two plaques commemorating Jane Austen's association with Lyme Regis in Jane Austen's Garden, which overlooks the beach where she bathed in 1804. (Author's collection)

19. The Cobb, Lyme Regis, Dorset

Featured in Jane Austen's Persuasion
Location: The Cobb, Lyme Regis, DTZ 3JJ
Map co-ordinates: 50°43′13.0″N 2°56′19.6″W; decimal: 50.720276, -2.938786

According to her letter written 14 September 1804, Jane Austen walked along the Cobb for an hour during her visit to Lyme Regis. The experience left such an impression upon her that when she wrote *Persuasion* eleven years later during 1815/16, she set one of the scenes on the Cobb. It is evident that Jane was writing from personal experience as she described the protagonists walking through the town:

> ... down the principal street almost hurrying into the water, the walk to the Cobb skirting round the pleasant little bay, which in the season, is animated with bathing-machines and company; the Cobb itself, its old wonders and new improvements, with the very beautiful line of cliffs stretching out to the east of the town.

It was on the Cobb that Jane Austen created the memorable scene of Lousia Musgrove's accident. Louisa jumped from the upper Cobb intending for Captain Wentworth to catch her, which he did so, but when she dashed back up to the upper Cobb and jumped again, he missed her and she fell onto the lower Cobb, seriously injuring herself.

There are three flights of steps along the Cobb. The first flight is too near to the land and the second flight was used to film this particular scene in the 1995 BBC adaptation. Known as Granny's Teeth because of the steps that protrude from the upper Cobb, it was built in 1816, ten years after Jane's visit to Lyme Regis, and so therefore Jane possibly visualised the scene taking place at the third flight of steps towards the end of the Cobb.

The Cobb, Lyme Regis, looking eastwards towards Charmouth. (Author's collection)

The Cobb, Lyme Regis, looking west towards Pinhay. (Author's collection)

The steps that Jane Austen may have visualised as the scene of Captain Wentworth's failure to catch Louisa Musgrove who accidently falls on the lower Cobb in *Persuasion.* (Author's collection)

20. No. 3 Green Park Buildings East, Bath

The Reverend George Austen died here

Location: Nos 20–39 Green Park Buildings, Bath, BA1 1HZ

Map co-ordinates: 51°22′49.7″N 2°22′04.0″W; decimal: 51.380469, -2.367768

Jane viewed two houses in Green Park Buildings on 5 May 1801, soon after the Austens' arrival in Bath with her uncle. She liked one of the houses but dismissed it as a place to live because of the 'dampness of the offices'.

Jane viewed other houses at Green Park Buildings two weeks later on 21 May 1801 and dampness remained a common problem, as she reported to Cassandra:

> Our views on G.P. Buildings seem all at an end; the observation of the damps still remaining in the offices of an [*sic*] house which has been only vacated a week, with reports of discontented families and putrid fevers has given the *coup de grace*. We have now nothing to view.

Despite the issue of dampness, Jane enthused about Green Park Buildings, probably because they had no other alternative houses to view and she thought that it was a possibility. 'We will at least have the pleasure of examining some of these putrefying houses again; they are so very desirable in size and situation in spending ten minutes within them.'

The houses on Green Park West are similar to the house that Jane Austen occupied on Green Park East, which was destroyed during the Second World War. The raised stone platform on which Green Park Buildings were built to prevent the houses from being flooded by water from the River Avon can be seen today. (Author's collection)

Four years later when the lease of No. 4 Sydney Place had expired the family moved into No. 3 Green Park Buildings East after their return from Lyme Regis during autumn 1804. Despite the dampness, it was affordable and closer to the centre of Bath for Jane's father to walk to. However, Green Park Buildings was close to the River Avon which was prone to flooding. The houses were built on a raised stone platform, which can be seen in Green Park, where the water from the river overspilled. The Austens moved here four years after being made aware of the 'putrid' fevers that previous residents had succumbed to when they viewed properties when they first arrived in Bath. Those putrid fevers would have tragic consequences for the Austen family when they moved into Green Park Buildings in 1804.

George Austen became ill and was suffering from fever, a condition that he had had since 1802, and which would be exacerbated once they moved to Green Park Buildings. Living in a damp house, close to a river that overspilled and with mosquitos present, may have brought on further fevers and contributed to his failing health. It is surmised that he may have been suffering from malaria while living here.

It was at No. 3 Green Park Buildings that George Austen, aged seventy-three, died on 21 January 1805 after suffering from a 'feverish complaint' which was 'a more violent attack from the first'.

Jane and her family would remain at No. 3 Green Park Gardens for a further three months until the lease expired in March 1805. The houses on the eastern side of Green Park Gardens, including No. 3, were destroyed by German bombs during the Second World War and no longer exist, although the western terrace remains and gives an idea of how Jane Austen's home looked.

21. Tombstone of the Reverend George Austen

Jane Austen's father was buried at St Swithin's Church, Walcot, Bath

Location: St Swithin's Church, The Paragon, Walcot, Bath, BA1 5LU

Map co-ordinates: 51°23′19.4″N 2°21′34.3″W; decimal: 51.388717, -2.359536

Jane's parents, George Austen and Cassandra Leigh, were married at her parish church of St Swithin's on 26 April 1764. The Reverend George Austen was regarded as gentry in the social hierarchy of Georgian society, but without wealth and an estate he was beneath the aristocratic and governing classes. He was able to supplement his income as a rector by farming and teaching pupils while living at Steventon Rectory, where he would prepare the latter for university. They were not affluent, but George earned a comfortable income which enabled him to raise and educate his family.

St Swithin's Church was rebuilt between 1771 and 1780 on the same site and is the church that exists today. Fifty years after George married Cassandra, he was buried in its crypt near to his father-in-law. Jane wrote to her brother Frank, 'The funeral is to be on Saturday at Walcot Church. The serenity of the corpse is most delightful. It preserves the sweet benevolent smile which always distinguished him.'

George Austen's tombstone was removed from the crypt to its current site in 1968 and in 2000 it was remounted and a plaque placed next to it, installed by the Jane Austen Society with support from the Bristol and Bath branch and the Jane Austen societies of North America and Australia.

Above left: The Reverend George Austen's tombstone and plaque inaugurated by the Jane Austen Society. When the church is closed the headstone and plaque can be seen through the railings in The Paragon. (Author's collection)

Above right: St Swithin's Church, Walcot, Bath. Fanny Burney, the renowned author admired by the Austens, was buried at Walcot church when she died in 1840. (Author's collection)

22. No. 25 Gay Street, Bath

Jane Austen lodged here

Location: 25 Gay Street, Bath, BA1 2BD

Map co-ordinates: 51°23′06.1″N 2°21′49.2″W; decimal: 51.385019, -2.363668

The death of George Austen meant that the income of Mrs Austen and her daughters had been substantially reduced. They were all dependent upon George Austen's annual pension of £600 and his passing had placed the women that he had left behind in financial crisis. Mrs Austen was left to live on £210 per year, which was interest earned from a family inheritance that she had invested, as well as interest earned on £1,000 inherited by Cassandra from Thomas Fowle, her late fiancé. It was fortunate that Jane and Cassandra's

Above left: No. 25 Gay Street. (Author's collection)

Above right: Although Jane Austen only lived briefly at No. 25 Gay Street, several doors to the south at No. 40 Gay Street there is a visitor centre dedicated to Bath's most famous resident. A mannequin of Jane welcomes visitors to the Jane Austen Centre in Bath. (Author's collection)

The Royal Crescent, Bath, which was close to Gay Street. In a letter dated 8 April 1805 Jane Austen mentions drinking tea at the Royal Crescent. (Author's collection)

brothers, Edward, James, Henry and Frank, were able to contribute, further raising their income to £460 per year to live on. This meant they could only afford one domestic servant instead of three servants.

On 25 March 1805, Mrs Austen, Jane and Cassandra moved into lodgings at No. 25 Gay Street, which was in a fashionable district in the centre of Bath. Jane considered moving to Gay Street in 1801 and mentioned that only part of the street was affordable: 'Gay Street would be too high, except only the lower house on the left-hand side as you ascend. Towards that my mother has no disinclination; it used to be lower rented than any other house in the row, from some inferiority in the apartments.'

The house at No. 25 Gay Street was smaller and needed only one maid. During April 1805, Martha Lloyd's mother died at Ibthrop, and she joined the Austens to live with them at this address. Martha could contribute to living expenses and if they pooled their resources and income, they could live comfortably. They did not live in Gay Street for too long, vacating the property during January 1806, possibly because they could not afford the rent.

Gay Street features in *Persuasion* with Admiral Croft finding accommodation in this location.

23. Stanford Cottage, Worthing, Sussex

Jane Austen's lodging during autumn 1805

Location: Stanford Cottage, Warwick Street, Worthing, BN11 3EZ

Map co-ordinates: 50°48′42.2″N 0°22′06.2″W; decimal: 50.811769, -0.368410

Grieving for the loss of the Reverend George Austen, Jane, Cassandra and their mother decided to spend autumn 1805 in Worthing, a small seaside resort in Sussex. Mrs Austen and Martha Lloyd stayed in Worthing for seven weeks before Jane and Cassandra arrived. Jane first mentioned staying here in a letter to Cassandra, who was at Goodnestone, Kent, on 26 August 1805, when she was with her brother at Godmersham Park and referred to her nephew Edward being ill: 'Unless he recovers his strength beyond what is now probable, his brothers will return to school without him, and he will be of the party to Worthing. If sea bathing should be recommended, he will be left there with us, but this is not thought likely to happen.' Edward recovered and Jane went to Goodnestone while Cassandra took Jane's place and stayed at Godmersham Park, with Jane writing, on 30 August, that the sisters' plan to visit London could 'injure our Worthing scheme'. Jane ended that letter with, 'We shall not be at Worthing so soon as we have been used to talk of, shall we? This will be no evil to us, and we are sure of my mother and Martha being happy together.'

It is not known when Jane and Cassandra eventually joined Mrs Austen and Martha in Worthing, but their niece Fanny Knight wrote to her governess that she would be joining them and would be staying at Mr Stanford's cottage on 15 September. Two days later, she left Godmersham Park, arriving at Worthing on 17 September.

Stanford Cottage, Worthing. (Author's collection)

The plaque commemorating Jane Austen's stay at Stanford Cottage. (Author's collection)

On 19 September, Fanny recorded that 'we dined at 4 and went to a raffle in the evening, where aunt Jane won and it amounted to 17s'. She also mentions walking with her aunt Jane on 20 September and attending church with her on Sunday 22 September, before Fanny left them and returned to Godmersham Park. It is surmised that the Austens remained in Worthing until December 1805.

Worthing would provide the setting for Jane Austen's final and unfinished novel entitled *Sanditon,* which she began writing twelve years after visiting the Sussex seaside resort.

Stanford Cottage was named after its owner, Edward Stanford (1768–1858), who was a tailor who sold hats and pianos. Today, the cottage stands in an alley south of Warwick Street and is now a Pizza Express which commemorates Jane Austen with paperback copies of her novels and images of her on the interior walls of the restaurant. In 2010, the Worthing Society unveiled a plaque that commemorates Jane Austen's visit.

24. Trim Street, Bath

The least desirable residence in Bath for the Austens

Location: Trim Street, Bath, BA11 1HB

Map co-ordinates: 51°22′57.6″N 2°21′41.8″W; decimal: 51.382662, -2.361604

Trim Street was named after George Trim, who built the street in 1707. At that time, the houses and shops in the street were fashionable. General James Wolfe was living at No. 5 when he received orders from Acting Prime Minister William Pitt the Elder to lead an expedition to capture Quebec in 1759. Forty years later, when the Austen family was looking for suitable accommodation, the street was a commercial quarter and considered less desirable. Mrs Austen preferred to live in the corner house at Chapel Row and Princes Street, but Jane wrote of her mother's reluctance to reside in Trim Street on 3 January 1801: 'In the meantime, she assures you that she will do everything to avoid Trim Street, although you have not expressed the fearful presentiment of it which was rather expected.'

The narrowness of the street and the close proximity of dwellings with chimneys that polluted the air quality, together with the lack of light and the non-existent views of the countryside, may have influenced the Austens' opinion that Trim Street was an unappealing place to live. Residing here may have been too claustrophobic for the Austens who had lived all their lives in a rural environment. Also, the buildings in Trim Street were a hundred years old.

Trim Street, according to Jane Austen, was to be avoided in 1801, but the Austens lived here temporarily in 1805. (Author's collection)

The Trim Street sign carved into the stone of one of the houses. (Author's collection)

After Jane's father had died, they had no option but to seek cheaper accommodation, and the final place where they stayed in Bath was in Trim Street, which they leased temporarily from January 1806, although the exact address in that street is unknown. The Austens lived in Trim Street for six months before relocating to Clifton, then a suburb of Bristol, on 2 July 1806. Jane did not savour living in Bath and was elated when she left the city, later writing to Cassandra, 'it will be two years tomorrow since we left Bath for Clifton with what happy feelings of Escape!'.

25. Stoneleigh Abbey, Warwickshire

Jane Austen visited Stoneleigh Abbey, July 1806

Location: Stoneleigh Abbey, Stoneleigh, Kenilworth, CV8 2SJ

Map co-ordinates: 52°20′30.1″N 1°32′40.4″W; decimal: 52.341706, -1.544568

After leaving Clifton, the Austen ladies visited Mrs Austen's cousin, the Reverend Thomas Leigh, at Adlestrop, Gloucestershire. During that visit, they received news that on 2 July 1806 the Honourable Mary Leigh had died. She had been the owner of Stoneleigh Abbey for twenty years and there were no children to inherit the vast estate. Therefore, an heir had to be found from distant cousins. The Reverend Thomas Leigh was one of the cousins and a potential beneficiary, so accompanied by Mrs Austen, Jane and Cassandra they went to Stoneleigh Abbey on 5 August 1806 to affirm his claim to the estate. Mrs Austen had a vested interest in that her brother James Leigh-Perrot would be next in line to inherit the estate.

It would take two years to resolve the matter. 'Yes, the Stoneleigh business is concluded,' wrote Jane on 21 November 1808. 'My aunt says as little as may be on the subject by way of information, and nothing at all by way of satisfaction.'

Stoneleigh Abbey was a Cistercian monastery built in 1155. In 1561, it was given to the Leigh family of which Jane's mother was a descendant. The Leigh family used the stones from the monastery that that was dissolved during the reign of Henry VIII to build the house that stands today. (Alamy)

There were legal ambiguities as to who should inherit Stoneleigh Abbey as there were other claimants within the family and James Leigh-Perrot agreed to waver his claim in return for a lump sum of £24,000 and an annuity of £2,000. Jane's aunt would have inherited Stoneleigh Abbey when the Reverend Thomas Leigh died in 1813 had her husband not agreed to this settlement. Jane would refer to the settlement in a letter written to Frank Austen, dated 3 July 1813, as 'a vile compromise' and that Thomas Leigh 'must have died the possessor of one of the finest estates in England, and of more worthless nephews and nieces than any private man in the United Kingdom'. Jane, Cassandra and their mother were on the list of beneficiaries of relatives in Mary Leigh's will who were made bequests of rings, bracelets and brooches.

Jane Austen would stay at Stoneleigh Abbey for five weeks and it was probably one of the largest houses that she resided in. It is believed that Jane Austen used Stoneleigh Abbey as a setting for the home of Mr Rushworth, Sotherton Court, in her novel *Mansfield Park*. In the novel, Sotherton Court needed much refurbishment, as did Stoneleigh Abbey. Rushworth described his dilapidated abode as 'a dismal old prison' to Mrs Norris, who disagreed in her response, 'Sotherton Court is the noblest old place in the world.'

The strongest indication that Austen used Stoneleigh Abbey as the setting for Sotherton Court in *Mansfield Park* is in the scene where Fanny Price is taken on a guided tour and describes the chapel in great detail. The similarities with the chapel at Stoneleigh Abbey are striking, including the crimson velvet cushions that can still be seen today: 'Fanny's imagination had prepared her for something grander than a mere spacious, oblong room, fitted up for the purpose of devotion; with nothing more striking or more solemn than the profusion of mahogany, and the crimson velvet cushions appearing over the ledge of the family gallery above.'

26. Juniper Berry Public House, Southampton

A plaque denotes this is the site of Jane Austen's home at Castle Square, Southampton

Location: Juniper Berry, Cement Terrace, Southampton, SO14 2EE

Map co-ordinates: 50°54′04.3″N 1°24′21.3″W; decimal: 50.901180, -1.405916

Jane's first letter from Southampton was written on 7 January 1807, but the location of her lodgings is unknown. It was not until March 1807 that she began detailing her address as Castle Square in her letters and it can be assumed that she moved into a house here on this site around that time.

Jane lived at Castle Square with her mother, Cassandra, Martha Lloyd and her brother Frank with his wife Mary Gibson, whom he married on 26 July 1806. By combining their incomes, they could afford better accommodation. It was close enough for her brother James and his wife to visit from Steventon and for her naval officer brother Frank to be near to Portsmouth and the Royal Navy dockyard. They leased the property from the Marquis of Lansdowne who lived opposite in his mock-Gothic castle. Frank was appointed commander of HMS *St Albans* during April 1807 and did not spend much time in the house.

As the Austens settled at Castle Square, they got to know people in Southampton and Jane wrote on 20 February 1807, 'we hear that we are envied our house by many people, and that the garden is the best in the town'.

Jane Austen lived in this property between 1807 and 1809 and now the Juniper Berry pub in Castle Square stands here. A plaque marking the site as once the home of Jane Austen is displayed on the pub wall in Cement Terrace. The garden stretched to the medieval town wall from where the New Forest could be seen looking westwards across Southampton

The plaque found on the wall of the Juniper Berry public house which marks the site of Jane Austen's home at Castle Square, Southampton. The medieval wall that skirted the bottom of her garden stands today and can be seen at the far end of the street in this photograph. (Author's collection)

Water. During the Georgian era, at high tide the sea would reach the base of the medieval wall. Today, the medieval wall overlooks reclaimed land on which a leisure facility and a shopping centre have been built. James Austen-Leigh remembered the house where Jane Austen lived when he visited her as a child:

> They resided in a commodious old-fashioned house in a corner of Castle Square ... My grandmother's [Mrs Austen] house had a pleasant garden, bounded on one side by the old city walls; the top of this wall was sufficiently wide to afford a pleasant walk, with an extensive view, easily accessible to ladies by steps.

When Jane Austen's sister-in-law Eliza (Elizabeth Bridges) died after giving birth to her eleventh child at Godmersham Park on 8 October 1808, Jane comforted her nephews Edward and George at Castle Square.

Jane Austen's last surviving letter written from Castle Square was dated 30 January 1809. The Austens left Southampton on 3 April 1809, staying first in Alton and then spending several weeks at Godmersham Park before moving into their new home at Chawton. The castle and Jane Austen's home were demolished during 1809 after the death of the Marquis of Lansdowne.

Jane Austen's home at Castle Square can be seen in the centre of this painting in front of the Marquis of Lansdowne's Gothic castle. (Author's collection)

The medieval wall and Juniper Bell public house (the timbered building) which marks the site of Jane Austen's home in Southampton. The wall was at the bottom of the garden and she could watch the tide coming in as it approached the base of the wall. (Author's collection)

27. The Dolphin Hotel, Southampton

Jane Austen danced in the ballroom

Location: 34–35 High Street, Southampton, SO14 2HN

Map co-ordinates: 50°54′00.2″N 1°24′13.8″W; decimal: 50.900059, -1.403829

The Dolphin Hotel was once a coaching inn called the Dolphin Inn, which, according to John Feltham in 1806, was one of 'the capital houses of entertainment'.

Assemblies and balls began to be held in the ballroom on the first floor from 1785. These events started on the first Tuesday in November and were every fortnight until the end of the winter season in April, beginning at 7 p.m. and ending at 11 p.m.

Jane Austen is reputed to have celebrated her eighteenth birthday in the ballroom of the Dolphin on 16 December 1793 with her brother Frank. Jane was staying with her cousins, the Butler-Harrisons, in St Mary's Street at the time. John Butler-Harrison served two terms as Mayor of Southampton during winter 1808–09.

According to Jane's letters, she attended two other dances at the Dolphin ballroom. Before the Austens moved from Southampton to Chawton, Jane wanted to attend as many

A plaque commemorating Jane Austen's association with the Dolphin Hotel, Southampton. (Author's collection)

balls as possible. She mentions in a letter, dated 9 December 1808, that she attended a ball and refers to her visit fifteen years previously which would be during 1793, the year of her eighteenth, which means that it is highly probable that the ball in 1808 took place at the Dolphin Inn.

> Our ball was rather more amusing than I expected, Martha liked it very much, and I did not gape till the last quarter of an hour. It was past nine before we were sent for, and not twelve when we returned. The room was tolerably full, and there were perhaps thirty couples of dancers. The melancholy part was, to see so many dozen young women standing by without partners, and each of them with two ugly shoulders. It was the same room in which we danced fifteen years ago. I thought it all over, and spite of the shame of being so much older, felt with thankfulness that I was quite as happy now as then.

As a single woman, Jane was content with her life and may have valued her independence. She could focus on enjoying quality time with her family, her mother, siblings, nephews and nieces, as well as the freedom to continue her writing. It is probable that she just enjoyed dancing and socialising without the aspiration of finding romance and a husband. While attending the ball at the Dolphin Hotel, she reported, 'You will not expect to hear that I was asked to dance, but I was – by the gentleman whom we met that Sunday with Captain D'Auvergne.' Jane gives the impression that it was an unusual occurrence at this time of life being to be asked to dance.

The Dolphin Hotel, Southampton. The two bow windows on the first floor are in what used to be the ballroom in which Jane Austen celebrated her eighteenth birthday. (Author's collection)

28. Jane Austen's House, Chawton, Hampshire

Jane Austen's home from 1809–17

Location: Jane Austen's House, Winchester Road, Chawton, GU34 1BA

Map co-ordinates: 51°07′58.9″N 0°59′20.0″W; decimal: 51.133037, -0.988899

The cottage at Chawton where Jane Austen lived between 1809 and 1817 stands a mile south of Alton, on a junction of two roads from Winchester and Gosport which led to London. The property was 300 years old when Jane moved into it and had once been a farmhouse. It was bought by the Knight family in 1769 and formed part of their Chawton estate. The cottage served as a pub called the New Inn and later became the home to an employee on Edward's Chawton estate, Mr Seward, who served as steward until he died prior to Jane Austen's arrival.

Chawton Cottage was inherited by Jane's brother Edward Knight, and he offered Jane, her mother, sister Cassandra and Martha Lloyd the choice of taking this property on the Chawton estate or one on his Godmersham estate. Jane's first reference to a potential move from Southampton to Chawton was in a letter to Cassandra, dated 24 October 1808:

> Of Chawton I think I can have nothing more to say, but that everything you say about it in the letter now before me will, I am sure, as soon as I am able to read it to her, make my mother consider the plan with more and more pleasure.

The cottage at Chawton was L-shaped, had two storeys, built of red-bricks and spacious with six bedrooms. The Austen ladies chose to remain in Hampshire and settled on Chawton Cottage, where Edward allowed them to live rent free. Mrs Austen, Jane, Cassandra and their friend Martha Lloyd took possession of the cottage on 7 July 1809. Enchanted by her new home, Jane wrote of her delight of living here in verses she sent to her brother Frank on 26 July 1809:

> Our Chawton home, how much we find,
> Already in it, to our mind;
> And how convinced, that when complete
> It will all other Houses beat.

The previous eight years, since leaving the family home at Steventon, had been an unsettling period for Jane, the family living in a series of rented properties. The move to Chawton Cottage ended that uncertainty and Jane could begin to take comfort in the security of a permanent home without financial concerns, as this verse suggests.

The house is of significant historic interest because it was here that Jane Austen revised, wrote and had published her six prominent works. *Sense and Sensibility*, *Pride and Prejudice* and *Northanger Abbey* had been written at Steventon but were revised at Chawton Cottage, while *Mansfield Park*, *Emma* and *Persuasion* were completely new works created in this building.

Above: Jane Austen's house in Chawton, Hampshire. (Author's collection)

Right: The plaque commemorating Jane Austen's home at Chawton. (Author's collection)

Below: The front of Jane Austen's house at Chawton, Hampshire. (Author's collection)

29. Jane Austen's Writing Table

Used by Jane Austen to write her novels

Location: Jane Austen's House, Winchester Road, Chawton, GU34 1BA

Map co-ordinates: 51°07′58.9″N 0°59′20.0″W; decimal: 51.133037, -0.988899

Jane could now concentrate on her writing and focus on getting her work published while living at Chawton cottage. She had three manuscripts for novels already written, *Elinor and Marianne, First Impressions* and *Susan,* which were all unpublished. Her first objective was to revise these books to improve them and obtain a better chance of getting them published. These books would be transformed into *Sense and Sensibility, Pride and Prejudice* and *Northanger Abbey.* At Chawton Cottage she was able to write three new novels, *Mansfield Park, Emma* and *Persuasion.*

This fragile twelve-sided mahogany table was used by Jane in the dining parlour of the cottage. She chose to write beside the window because of the natural light and she could watch proceedings in the village. Her mother, sister and Martha Lloyd supported Jane in her literary endeavours but when servants or visitors entered the dining parlour, she would be alerted by the creaking door and conceal her work beneath some blotting paper on the table. James Austen-Leigh wrote: 'She was careful that her occupation should not be suspected by servants, or visitors, or any such persons beyond her own family party. She wrote upon small sheets of paper which could be easily put away, or covered with a piece of blotting paper.'

William Littleworth worked as a servant in the Austen household and the family gave him the writing table after Jane's death. The Knight family obtained possession of the table in 1913, presenting it to the Jane Austen Society in 1957 for public display in the cottage.

Above: Jane Austen's writing table in the room where she sometimes wrote her novels. (Alamy)

Left: Jane Austen's writing desk, positioned in the dining parlour in her home at Chawton where she worked on six of her novels. (Author's collection)

30. Chawton House, Hampshire

Home of Edward Knight, brother of Jane Austen

Location: Chawton House, Gosport Road, Chawton, GU34 1SJ

Map co-ordinates: 51°07′44.3″N 0°59′27.8″W; decimal: 51.128971, -0.991061

A manor house has existed on this site since 1224. John Knight acquired the estate, and construction of the house that stands today was completed in 1588. Jane's brother Edward Knight inherited Chawton House and would visit the estate twice a year to attend to his affairs.

When Edward gave Jane, Cassandra and their mother use of the cottage at Chawton in 1809, he had leased Chawton House to tenants. During spring 1813, Edward brought his family to live at Chawton House while his home, Godmersham Park, was being refurbished. Jane was elated for in a letter sent to her brother Frank, on 3 July 1813, she wrote: 'The pleasure to us of having them here is so great that if we were not the best creatures in the world we should not deserve it. We go on in the most comfortable way, very frequently dining together, and always meeting in some part of every day.'

The cottage at Chawton is a ten-minute walk from Chawton House and Jane would regularly visit her brother, and his family would make the short trip to the cottage. On 18 November 1814, Jane wrote, 'Aunt Cass. and I dine at the Great House today. We shall be a snug half dozen.' Her niece Caroline Austen remembered her aunts Jane and Cassandra's regular visits to Chawton House:

> After luncheon my aunts generally walked out; sometimes they went to Alton for shopping, often, one or the other of them to the 'Great House', as it was then called, in order, when a brother was inhabiting it, to make a visit, or, if the house were standing empty, they liked to stroll about the grounds, sometimes to Chawton Park, a noble beech wood, just within a walk.

Chawton House. (Author's collection)

Jane's niece Fanny Knight would frequently record in her diary 'we dined at the cottage' or 'the cottage dined here'. Jane would attend family gatherings in the dining room of Chawton House. Fanny Knight recorded that one morning during June 1813 Jane read *Pride and Prejudice* to the family at Chawton House.

Above: The dining room at Chawton House where Jane Austen dined with her family. (Author's collection)

Left: An alcove in the Oak Room where Jane Austen would sit, sew and read. (Author's collection)

31. Jane Austen Statue, St Nicholas Church, Chawton

Perception of Jane Austen

Location: St Nicholas Church, Chawton, Hampshire, GU34 1SJ

Map co-ordinates: 51°07′43.0″N 0°59′24.1″W; decimal: 51.128599, -0.990034

Situated on her brother's estate at Chawton, St Nicholas Church was the closest church to the cottage where the Austens lived. From 1809, Jane Austen worshipped here until her death in 1817. The church that stands today was rebuilt after the one that Jane knew was destroyed by fire in 1871. If Jane Austen had not been buried in Winchester Cathedral, it is probable that she would have been interred in the churchyard of St Nicholas Church, Chawton, where her mother and sister Cassandra were later buried.

Outside St Nicholas Church there is a bronze statue of Jane Austen, a smaller version of the one that stands in Basingstoke. Jane is depicted looking in the direction of her cottage in the village. It can also be interpreted as Jane on her regular walks from Chawton Cottage to her brother's home at Chawton House or going to church on a Sunday. The inscription on the plinth simply reads 'Jane Austen worshipped here, 1809–1817'.

Jane's brother Henry Austen provided an insight into Jane's appearance, her character and how she sounded in the following tribute:

> Her stature was that of true elegance. It could not have been increased without exceeding the middle height. Her carriage and deportment were quiet, yet graceful. Her features were separately good. The assemblage produced an unrivalled expression of that cheerfulness, sensibility, and benevolence, which were her real characteristics. Her complexion was of the finest texture. It might with truth be said that her blood spoke through her modest cheek. Her voice was extremely sweet. She delivered herself with fluency and precision. Indeed, she was formed for elegant and rational society, excelling in conversation as much as composition.

The Jane Austen statue in the grounds of St Nicholas Church, Chawton. (Author's collection)

32. Portrait of Jane Austen

An engraving taken from an original drawing by Jane's sister Cassandra

Location: The original drawing is displayed at the National Portrait Gallery, St Martin's Place, London, WC2H 0HE. Room 5, Floor 3

Map co-ordinates: 51°30′34.2″N 0°07′39.6″W; decimal: 51.509510, -0.127678

Cassandra Austen drew a pencil and watercolour portrait of her sister Jane around 1810. It is the only image drawn from life that shows Jane Austen's face. The two sisters shared such a close bond, which makes this image of Jane Austen very personal. After Jane died, Cassandra wrote of the devastation that she felt following her sister's death to their niece Fanny Knight:

> I have lost a treasure, such a sister, such a friend, as never can have been surpassed. She was the sun of my life, the gilder of every pleasure, the soother of every sorrow; I had not a thought concealed from her, and it is as if I have lost a part of myself. I loved her only too well.

Cassandra's portrait was used by their nephew Edward Austen-Leigh to form the basis of this engraving. He included it in his *A Memoir of Jane Austen*, published in 1870. The engraving also features on the £10 banknote introduced in 2017, the bicentennial year of Jane's death. The original drawing was purchased by the National Portrait Gallery, London, during 1947 and is displayed there.

A portrait of Jane Austen adapted from a drawing by Cassandra Austen. (Author's collection) (Austen-Leigh, Emma, Jane Austen and Lyme Regis) (Spottiswoode, Ballantyne and Co. Ltd, 1944)

33. The Dining Parlour, Chawton Cottage

The room where the Austens ate and Jane wrote

Location: Jane Austen's House, Winchester Road, Chawton, GU34 1BA

Map co-ordinates: 51°07′58.9″N 0°59′20.0″W; decimal: 51.133037, -0.988899

As well as writing her novels in the corner of the parlour, Jane Austen would eat meals there. Breakfast would be taken between 9 and 10 in the morning. While at Godmersham, Jane confirmed that she ate breakfast at 10 a.m. As part of her household chores, it was Jane's responsibility to make the family breakfast and to administer supplies of tea, sugar and wine.

Lunch would be eaten around midday. Dinner was the main meal of the day and in previous centuries it would take place during the middle of the day when it could be cooked and eaten in daylight. By the eighteenth century, the higher echelons of society began to dine later in the day. According to a letter that Jane wrote in 1798, while living in Steventon, to Cassandra, who was at Godmersham Park, 'we dine now at half-past three and have done dinner, I suppose, before you begin. We drink tea at half-past six. I am afraid you will despise us.'

By December 1808, while living at Castle Square, Southampton, and a year before moving to Chawton, Jane wrote that 'we never dine now till five'.

While living in Chawton, people travelling in carriages passing by the cottage could look inside through the window of the dining parlour where Jane wrote and the family ate. Shortly after they moved into the cottage, Mrs Knight wrote, on 26 October 1809, 'I heard of the Chawton party looking very comfortable at breakfast from a gentleman who was travelling by their door in a Post-chaise about ten days ago.'

The dining parlour, Jane Austen's House, Chawton. Jane would write at her table in the corner of the room near the window. (Author's collection)

34. The Drawing Room, Chawton Cottage

The centre of daily life in the Austen household

Location: Jane Austen's House, Winchester Road, Chawton, GU34 1BA

Map co-ordinates: 51°07′58.9″N 0°59′20.0″W; decimal: 51.133037, -0.988899

As other members of the household were tending to their early chores, Jane practised the piano in the drawing room before she prepared breakfast. According to Caroline Austen:

> Aunt Jane began the day with music, for which I conclude she had a natural taste, as she thus kept it up, though she had no one to teach, and was never induced (as I have heard) to play in company, and none of her family cared much for it. I suppose that she might not trouble them she chose her practising time before breakfast, when she could have the room to herself. She practised regularly every morning. She played very pretty tunes I thought, and I liked to stand by her and listen to her. Much that she played was from manuscript copies written out by herself.

Jane was the most musically talented in the family, although it would appear, according to Caroline Austen, that the family were not too enamoured by music. However, the purpose of purchasing the piano was for playing for Jane's own pleasure and when her nieces

The drawing Room, Jane Austen's House, Chawton. The bookcase belonged to the Reverend George Austen when he lived at Steventon Rectory. (Alamy)

and nephews visited Chawton Cottage. Her nephew James Austen-Leigh did appreciate Jane's efforts to entertain and recalled her impromptu performances, which most likely took place in this drawing room, 'Jane herself was fond of music, and had a sweet voice, both in singing and conversation ... In the evening she would sometimes sing, to her own accompaniment.'

It was a pastime that was calming for the mind and through the character Anne Elliot, in the novel *Persuasion*, we get a sense of what playing the piano meant to Jane: 'while her fingers were mechanically at work, proceeding for half an hour together, equally without error, and without consciousness'.

Jane would play the piano in the drawing room until 9 a.m. and then she would prepare breakfast. After breakfast she would return to the drawing room for the remainder of the morning to carry out other chores such as mending and sewing clothes while entertaining visitors. During the evenings, the Austen women would use this room to write letters, read to each other, play parlour games or move the furniture aside and dance. It was in this room that Jane Austen read from one of the first published copies of *Pride and Prejudice* to her family for the first time on 28 January 1813. Her brother Henry testified that, 'She read aloud with very great taste and effect. Her own works, probably, were never heard to so much advantage as from her own mouth; for she partook largely in all the best gifts of the comic muse.'

A bookcase belonging to the Reverend George Austen and a pair of chairs made by cabinetmaker George Hepplewhite, furniture from Steventon Rectory, are displayed in the drawing room at Chawton Cottage.

35. No. 74 High Street, Alton, Hampshire

Home of Jane Austen's apothecary and surgeon

Location: 74 High Street, Alton, Hampshire, GU34 1EZ

Map co-ordinates: 51°08′51.8″N 0°58′37.9″W; decimal: 51.147730, -0.977195

Mr Newman was an apothecary who lived at No. 74 High Street, in Alton. Jane visited Newman with her friend Miss Beckford during February 1811. Miss Beckford lived at Basing Park in Hampshire and was mentioned in Jane's letters. Jane wrote the following

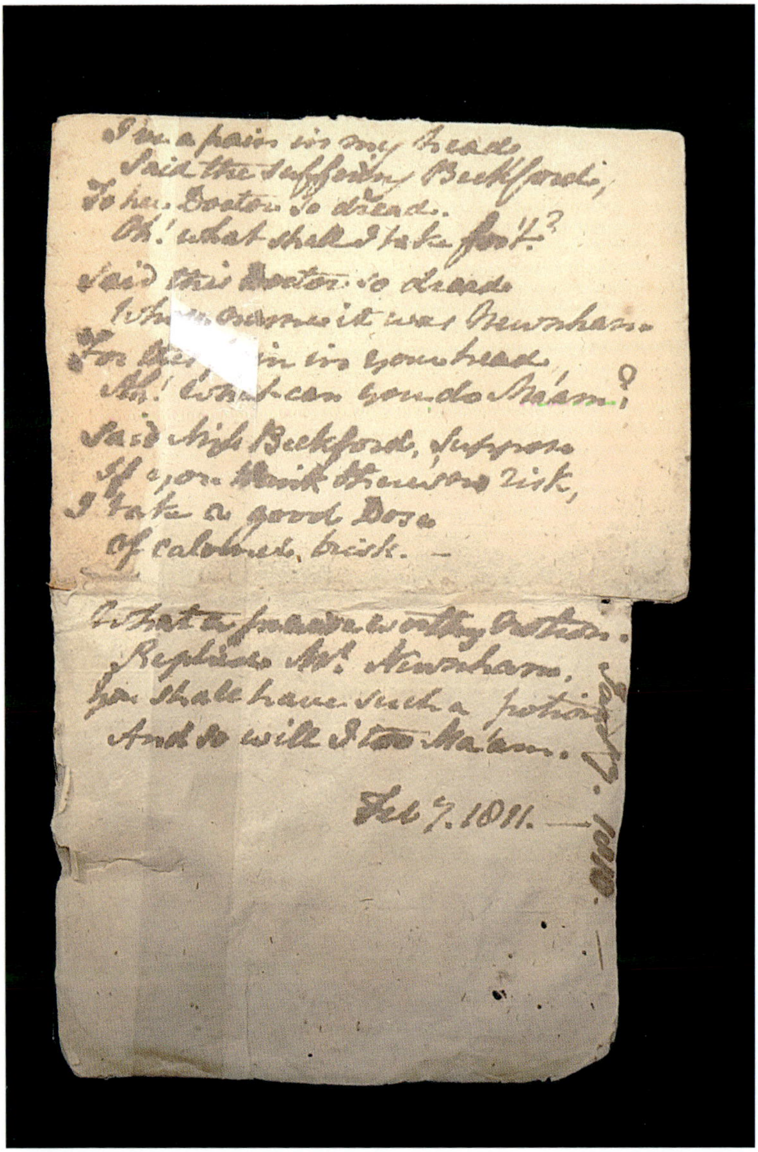

I've a pain in my head
Said the suffering Beckford;
To her Doctor so dread.
Oh! what shall I take for't?

Said this Doctor so dread
Whose name it was Newnham.
For this pain in your head
Ah! What can you do Ma'am?

Said Miss Beckford, Suppose
If you think there's no risk,
I take a good Dose
Of calomel brisk. —

What a praiseworthy notion.
Replied Mr. Newnham,
You shall have such a potion
And so will I too Ma'am.

Feb 7. 1811. —

The poem that Jane Austen wrote about Mr Newman is on display at the Winchester City Museum. (Author's collection, courtesy of Hampshire Cultural Trust)

humorous verse in four stanzas about the visit to Mr Newman, whom she refers to with trepidation and dismay as Newnham:

I've a pain in my head
Said the suffering Beckford,
To her Doctor so dread
Oh! What shall I take for it?

Said this Doctor so dread
Whose name if was Newnham,
For this pain in your head
Ah! What can you do Ma'am?

Said Miss Beckford, Suppose
If you think there's no risk
I take a good Dose
Of Calomel Brisk.

What a praiseworthy notion
Replied Mr. Newnham.
You shall have such a potion
And so will I too Ma'am.

No. 74 High Street, Alton, where Mr Newman the apothecary practised. (Author's collection)

36. Jane Austen's Letter to Cassandra, 25 April 1811

One of many regular correspondences written by Jane Austen to her sister

Location: British Library, 96 Euston Road, London, NW1 2DB

Map co-ordinates: 51°31′43.5″N 0°07′38.1″W; decimal: 51.528758, -0.127235

Given that Jane belonged to a large family who were living in Hampshire, Kent, London and, in the case of her brothers Frank and Charles, serving in the Royal Navy, they regularly communicated via letter.

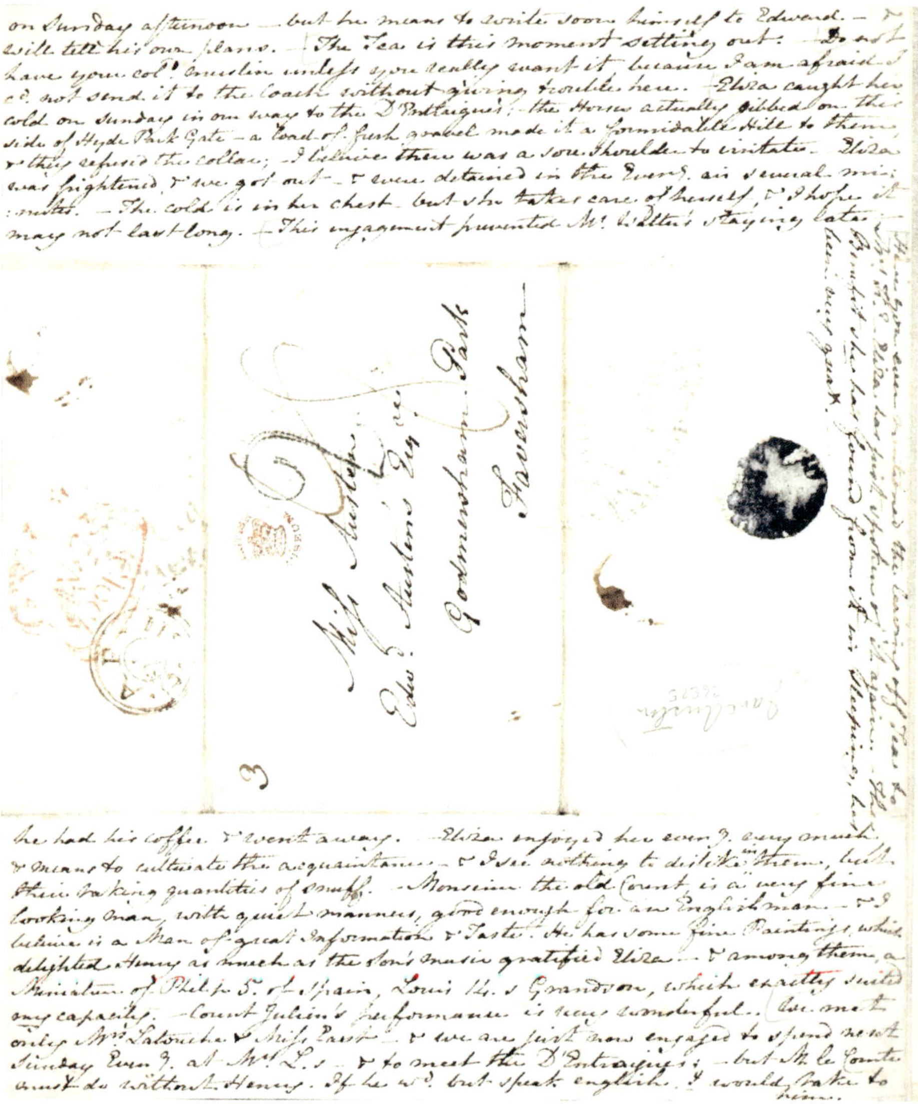

on Sunday afternoon — but he means to write soon himself to Edward. — & will tell his own plans. — The Tea is this moment setting out. — Do not have your col.d muslin unless you really want it, because I am afraid I c.d not send it to the Coach without giving trouble here. — Eliza caught her cold on Sunday in our way to the D'Entraigues; the Horses actually gibbed on this side of Hyde Park Gate — a load of fresh gravel made it a formidable Hill to them, & they refused the collar; — I believe there was a sore shoulder to irritate. — Eliza was frightened & we got out — & were detained in the Even.g air several minutes. — The cold is in her chest — but she takes care of herself, & I hope it may not last long. — This engagement prevented Mr. Walter's staying late — he had his coffee & went away. — Eliza enjoyed her even.g very much & means to cultivate the acquaintance — & I see nothing to dislike in them, but their taking quantities of snuff. — Monsieur the old Count, is a very fine looking man, with quiet manners, good enough for an Englishman — & I believe is a Man of great Information & Taste. He has some fine Paintings, which delighted Henry as much as the Son's music gratified Eliza — & among them, a Miniature of Philip 5. of Spain, Louis 14.s Grandson, which exactly suited my capacity. — Count Julien's performance is very wonderful. — We met only Mrs. Latouche & Miss East — & we are just now engaged to spend next Sunday Even.g at Mrs. L.s — & to meet the D'Entraigues; — but M. le Comte must do without Henry. If he w.d but speak english, I would take to him.

Miss Austen
Edw.d Austen's Esq.re
Godmersham Park
Faversham

Jane Austen's letter to Cassandra, 25 April 1811. (From the British Library Archives)

Jane shared a close relationship with her sister Cassandra. When they were separated, they regularly sent letters to each other while visiting friends or family. After Jane's death, in an effort to protect her sister's privacy, Cassandra destroyed many of her letters which were believed to have contained Jane's personal opinions about persons, including relatives and friends, which may have caused offence. Cassandra protected Jane's privacy and reputation as well as the sensitivities of people that she wrote about.

Only 161 letters survived Cassandra's censorship and these originate from those compiled by Lord Brabourne, their great-great-nephew. He also possessed letters written to his mother, Fanny Knight, whom Jane corresponded with when she was a girl, and others she wrote to her other niece Anna Austen. These letters are of significant historic importance as they provide an insight into the life of Jane Austen.

It was customary to write the letter on a large sheet of paper which was folded in four places. Envelopes did not exist at that time, so the letter would also serve as an envelope with some space reserved for the address and finally being sealed with wax. Stamps were not introduced until 1840 and during Jane's lifetime letters were sent and paid for by the recipient on receipt with the cost determined by how many sheets the letter contained and the distance covered to deliver it. The cost of sending a single sheet ranged from 4*d* to 1*s* 6*d* depending upon the distance to the recipient. If the letter exceeded an ounce, the cost would be multiplied by four and an additional sheet of paper would be regarded as two letters and charged double.

To reduce costs, Jane would attempt to fit as many words as possible to one page in her letters, using small writing in neat straight lines to utilise the space available.

The first of the surviving letters that Jane wrote was dated 9 January 1796 when she was aged twenty-one. The letters feature commentary on domestic matters, clothes worn, food that was eaten and people that they encountered. Accounts of balls where she lists dancing partners amongst her social circle are also included.

This letter was written by Jane Austen to her sister Cassandra on 25 April 1811 from No. 64 Sloane Street when she visited her brother Henry, while Cassandra was staying with their brother Edward at Godmersham Park.

37. No. 64 Sloane Street, London

Site of house where Jane Austen stayed in 1811

Location: No. 64 Sloane Street, London, SW1X 9SH

Map co-ordinates: 51°29′51.2″N 0°09′32.7″W; decimal: 51.497548, -0.159094

Henry Austen and his wife Eliza moved into No. 64 Sloane Street during 1809–13. Jane stayed with her brother at this address on various occasions. The house was three storeys high, including an attic, and in 1897 the house was refaced and refurbished, so although it was the original house, it has been rebuilt since Jane Austen's lifetime. The property formed part of the Hans Town development in the district known as Belgravia, a rural village surrounded by fields outside London during the 1780s. Jane would venture into the capital on shopping excursions with her sister-in-law. In a letter written on 18 April 1811, Jane wrote, 'If the weather permits, Eliza and I walk into London this morning.'

With Henry's assistance, Jane was able to find a publisher willing to publish *Sense and Sensibility*. Thomas Egerton was based at Military Library, Whitehall, London. Egerton

Jane Austen stayed with her brother Henry at No. 64 Sloane Street between 1809 and 1813. (Author's collection)

published the novel at his own expense on the provision that if the book did not sell well, Jane would pay for any losses incurred. The purpose of her visit to No. 64 Sloane Street during April 1811 was to review and correct proofs of *Sense and Sensibility* before it was printed for publication. Henry supported Jane in getting the novel printed.

The three external walls of the octagonal rooms on the ground, first and second floors can be seen by looking at the rear of No. 64 Sloane Street from Hans Street. Although the front façade has been renovated, the rear of the building has retained the Georgian architecture that would have been familiar to Jane Austen. Here Henry and Eliza Austen hosted a dinner party on 25 April 1811. This social function took part in the drawing room at the rear of the house, for Jane wrote, 'We were sixty-six – which was considerably more than Eliza had expected and quite enough to fill the back drawing-room and leave a few scattered about in the other and in the passage.' The back drawing room that Jane refers to in this letter was on one of the floors at the rear of No. 64 Sloane Street and is visible today from Hans Street.

Jane stayed at No. 64 Sloane Street between 22 April and 27 May 1813 and cared for Eliza during her final illness. She would comfort Henry when Eliza died on 25 April 1813.

The rear of No. 64, as seen from Hans Street, has retained its Georgian façade. On one of the floors Jane Austen attended a party hosted by her brother Henry Austen on 25 April 1811. (Author's collection)

38. Jane Austen's Muslin Shawl

An example of Jane Austen's needlework

Location: Jane Austen's House, Winchester Road, Chawton, GU34 1BA

Map co-ordinates: 51°07′58.9″N 0°59′20.0″W; decimal: 51.133037, -0.988899

During the Georgian era, needlework was a skill taught in most households and Jane would have learnt from her mother how to sew from an early age. Jane was reputed to have been proficient at stitching. The Austen ladies were self-sufficient and made clothes for themselves and their family. The only reference that Jane makes regarding her needlework skills is in a letter written on 1 September 1796 to Cassandra from her brother Edward's

A muslin shawl made by Jane Austen is displayed at the Jane Austen House, Chawton. (Author's collection)

The lid of an ivory spool case engraved with Jane Austen's initials, on display at Winchester City Museum. (Author's collection, courtesy of Hampshire Cultural Trust)

first home at Rowley, Kent, in which she states that they are 'all very busy making shirts, and I am proud to say that I am the neatest worker of the party'.

Jane's niece Anna wrote that her aunts would regularly sit together and make clothes for the less affluent members of their community. Another niece, Caroline, confirmed that as well as preparing breakfast, Jane would spend the mornings at work in the drawing room at Chawton sewing: 'She was fond of work, and was a great adept at overcast and satin-stitch – the peculiar delight of that day.'

Examples of Jane Austen's needlework exist. A white muslin shawl that she embroidered with satin-stitch crosses is displayed in the Jane Austen Museum in Chawton. Jane made her clothes in alignment with the fashions that she would see at assemblies and balls. Observing the clothes of other women would inspire her designs and Cassandra would also give sisterly advice. In a letter written on 18 December 1798 Jane writes of her positive influence:

> I have changed my mind, and changed the trimmings of my cap this morning; they are now such as you suggested. I felt as if I strayed from your directions, and I think it makes me look more like Lady Conyngham now than it did before, which is all that one lives for now. I believe I shall make my new gown like my robe, but the back of the latter is all in a piece with the tail, and will seven yards enable me to copy it in that respect?

39. No. 10 Henrietta Street, London

Jane Austen stayed here in 1813–14

Location: 10 Henrietta Street, London, WC2E 8PS

Map co-ordinates: 51°30′40.0″N 0°07′25.2″W; decimal: 51.511110, -0.123652

Jane's beloved brother Henry Austen was the entrepreneurial member of the family. In 1806, Henry established a bank named Austen, Maude and Tilson in London. This building at No. 10 Henrietta Street housed Henry Austen's bank. After the death of Eliza, he focused on work and lived in the chambers above the offices of the bank, which is situated close to Covent Garden. Jane Austen stayed with Henry in this building on 15 and 16 September 1813 for she wrote:

> We were accommodated in Henrietta Street. Henry was so good to find room for his three nieces and myself in his house. ... No. 10 is made very comfortable with cleaning and painting, and the Sloane Street furniture. The front room upstairs is an excellent dining and common sitting parlour, and the smaller one behind will sufficiently answer his purpose as a drawing room.

Above: During April 1999, the Jane Austen Society and the City of Westminster Council erected a green plaque at No. 10 Henrietta Street to commemorate Jane Austen's stay in this building during 1813–14. (Author's collection)

Left: No. 10 Henrietta Street, London. (Author's collection)

On arrival at No. 10 Henrietta Street, Madame Bigion (also referred to as Bigeon) had prepared 'a comfortable dinner of soup, fish, bouillee, partridges and an apple tart'.

While staying here, Jane would buy tea from Twining's. On 6 March 1814, she refers to the tea seller in a letter: 'I am sorry to hear that there has been a rise in tea. I do not mean to pay Twining till later in the day, when we may order a fresh supply.'

The entrance to Twining's at 216 The Strand, where Jane Austen bought tea. (Author's collection)

40. Theatre Royal, Drury Lane, London

Jane Austen regularly enjoyed the theatre

Location: Catherine Street, London, WC2B 5JF

Map co-ordinates: 51°30′45.8″N 0°07′14.1″W; decimal: 51.512707, -0.120578

Four theatres have stood on this site since 1660, and the rebuilding of the current theatre was completed in 1809. It was patronised by Jane Austen when it was regarded as a fashionable new theatre. The plays staged changed each month and there were no long runs for individual productions.

Jane Austen saw the esteemed actor Edmund Kean's performance as Shylock in William Shakespeare's *The Merchant of Venice* at Drury Lane Theatre. On 2 March 1815, she wrote of her excitement at seeing that performance and her desire to get as close to the stage as possible: 'Places are secured for Drury Lane for Saturday, but so great is the rage for seeing Kean that only a third and fourth row could be got; as it is in a front box, however I hope we shall do pretty well.'

After seeing Kean's performance as Shylock three days later on 5 March 1814, Jane wrote that 'we were quite satisfied with Kean. I cannot imagine better acting, but the part was too short; and excepting him and Miss Smith, and she did not quite answer my expectation, the parts were ill filled and the play heavy.'

The Theatre Royal, Drury Lane, London. (Author's collection)

41. HMS *Victory*

Captain Frank Austen, brother of Jane Austen, dined aboard with Nelson before the Battle of Trafalgar

Location: Portsmouth Historic Dockyard, Victory Gate, HM Naval Base, Portsmouth, PO1 3LJ
Map co-ordinates: 50°47′55.9″N 1°06′25.8″W; decimal: 50.798870, -1.107163

Frank and Charles Austen served on vessels which were similar to Vice-Admiral Lord Horatio Nelson's flagship at the Battle of Trafalgar. Both brothers established illustrious careers in the Royal Navy. Jane was immensely proud of her brothers and closely monitored their career progressions.

In February 1805, Captain Frank Austen was appointed commander of the larger third-rate warship HMS *Canopus,* which carried eighty-four guns. In a letter written in early 1805, Nelson described Austen:

> You can rely upon my every attention in my power to Captain Austen. I hope to see him alongside a French 80-gun ship, and he cannot be better placed than in the *Canopus,* which was once a French Admiral's ship, and struck me. Captain Austen, I knew a little of before; he is an excellent young man.

HMS *Victory* at Portsmouth Historic Dockyard. (Alamy)

The dining room aboard HMS *Victory* where Captain Frank Austen attended a dinner on 29 September 1805. During the evening, Vice-Admiral Lord Horatio Nelson discussed his plans for the Battle of Trafalgar. (Alamy)

Eighteen days before the Battle of Trafalgar, Captain Frank Austen dined with Nelson in the dining room aboard HMS *Victory* and was told that HMS *Canopus* would be sent to Gibraltar for replenishment. To be sent away from the British fleet before the impending engagement at Trafalgar was a major disappointment for Frank. He wrote to his wife Mary, 'You, perhaps, may not feel this so forcibly as I do, and in your satisfaction at my having avoided the danger of battle may not much regret my losing the credit of having contributed to gain a victory; not so myself.'

Jane featured the ships her brothers served aboard in her novels. 'By the bye shall you object to my mentioning the *Elephant* in it, and two or three other ships?' she asked Frank Austen on 3 July 1813. 'I have done it, but it shall not stay to make you angry. They are only just mentioned.' Jane placed William Price as second lieutenant aboard HMS *Thrush* in *Persuasion* and also mentions the *Canopus*. Her brother Charles Austen served aboard HMS *Endymion* in 1801 as a lieutenant and Jane refers to this warship in *Mansfield Park*.

42. The Landport Gate, Old Portsmouth

Featured in Jane Austen's Mansfield Park

Location: St George's Road, Portsmouth, PO1 2EW

Map co-ordinates: 50°47′36.4″N 1°06′03.9″W; decimal: 50.793450, -1.101087

Landport Gate, situated in St George's Road, was built in 1760 to a design by Nicholas Hawksmoor. Constructed from Portland stone, it was the principal route into the fortified town of Portsmouth until 1875. Earthen ramparts as high as the gate were positioned either side of it with a drawbridge and moat in front of it. Landport Gate is the only surviving town gate and is in its original position.

Although there is no written evidence of Jane Austen visiting Portsmouth, it is believed that she did visit the naval port because of her knowledge of various locations and the fact that her brothers Frank and Charles were serving officers in the Royal Navy. Her cousin Eliza de Feuillide insinuates in a letter to Philadelphia Walter soon after Charles Austen entered the Royal Naval Academy in Portsmouth in July 1791 that the family may have accompanied him on his journey to Portsmouth: 'As to Cassandra it is very probable as you observe that some son of Neptune may have obtained her approbation as she probably experienced much homage from these very gallant gentlemen during her aquatic excursions. I hear her sister and herself are two of the prettiest girls in England.' Although Portsmouth is not mentioned, the reference to an 'aquatic excursion', the expectation that Cassandra will attract the attention of some eligible young naval officer and the prospect of receiving homage from 'very gallant gentlemen' together with the comment about the

The Landport Gate, Portsmouth. (Author's collection)

The Ramparts, Old Portsmouth. Jane Austen may have walked along these ramparts because she referred to Fanny Price and Mr Crawford strolling upon them in *Mansfield Park*. (Author's collection)

attractiveness of Cassandra and Jane at a time when Charles entered the Royal Naval Academy suggests that they accompanied their brother.

It is highly probable that Jane Austen visited Portsmouth and she accurately mentioned the only entrance into Portsmouth and its drawbridge, which can only be Landport Gate, in *Mansfield Park* when Fanny Price approached 'the environs of Portsmouth ...They passed the drawbridge, and entered the town.'

43. Jane Austen Plaque, Site of No. 23 Hans Place, London

Jane stayed here with her brother Henry Austen

Location: No. 23 Hans Place, London, SW1X 0JY

Map co-ordinates: 51°29′49.7″N 0°09′38.8″W; decimal: 51.497127, -0.160786

Henry Austen moved to this house at No. 23 Hans Place, London, during 1814. Jane visited this address for the first time on 22 August 1814. The property in which Jane stayed still exists on this site but during 1884 it was refurbished and encased within a new building with a Victorian façade.

During 1815, it was from No. 23 Hans Place that Henry conducted negotiations with the publisher John Murray about publishing Jane's novels. Jane was fond of Henry and he was proud of his sister's literary endeavours. He had supported her in getting her work published, but he also revealed the secret that she was the author of *Sense and Sensibility* and *Pride and Prejudice* to his physician.

Jane stayed here for a longer period from 4 October 1815 while *Emma* was being prepared for publication. At the same time, Henry succumbed to a severe illness and Jane cared for him for the following three months until he recovered. Her relatives believed that the stress endured while caring for her ill brother and concern for his collapsed business had sapped her strength and impacted on her own health. This marked the beginning of a downward spiral which would eventually lead to her own demise.

Above: The plaque commemorating Jane Austen's visit to No. 23 Hans Place. (Author's collection)

Right: No. 23 Hans Place, London, the site of the home of Henry Austen. Jane Austen stayed here in 1814–15. The building was refaced during 1884. (Author's collection)

44. The London Premises of John Murray

The office of Jane Austen's publisher

Location: No. 50 Albemarle Street, London, W1S 4BD

Map co-ordinates: 51°30′28.9″N 0°08′27.1″W; decimal: 51.508028, -0.140869

During 1815, Thomas Egerton was reluctant to issue a second edition of *Mansfield Park,* which may have motivated Jane Austen to seek another publisher. She also had another novel entitled *Emma,* which she had begun writing in December 1813. William Gifford, the editor of the *Quarterly Review,* had read *Emma* and recommended the work to publisher John Murray, who owned the *Quarterly Review* and had been publishing from No. 50 Albemarle Street since 1812.

John Murray was the leading publisher of the day and had issued the works of Lord Byron, Walter Scott and Robert Southey. Henry Austen negotiated on behalf of his sister with Murray, and it is likely that both he and Jane visited John Murray at his office in Albemarle Street. When he became ill, Henry continued the negotiations in a letter from No. 23 Hans Place to Murray on 19 October 1815 despite experiencing difficulties holding a pen. In that letter he disagreed with Murray's critique of *Emma,* and with great subtlety challenged him on the amount that was being offered for its copyright.

Murray offered Jane £450 for *Emma,* together with the copyright of *Sense and Sensibility* and *Mansfield Park.* Henry Austen acted as Jane's agent and John Murray published *Emma* and a second edition of *Mansfield Park* on a profit-sharing basis.

While in London on 15 October 1815, Jane wrote, 'Mr Murray's letter is come. He is a rogue of course, but a civil one … He sends more praise than I expected.'

John Murray's office is still based at No. 50 Albemarle Street, London. (Author's collection)

45. Statue of King George IV, London

Jane Austen's royal admirer

Location: Trafalgar Square (north-east corner), London, WC2N 5DN

Map co-ordinates: 51°30′30.1″N 0°07′39.2″W; decimal: 51.508357, -0.127568

George, Prince of Wales had been acting as Prince Regent since 1811 when his father, King George III, became incapacitated and unable to rule. He would establish a reputation for his extravagance, excess drinking, gluttony and overindulgence in debauchery with many mistresses. He ascended the throne as King George IV after the death of his father in 1820.

A doctor named Matthew Baillie, who attended Henry Austen at No. 23 Hans Place, served as a physician to the Prince Regent. Baillie told Jane that the Prince Regent admired her novels and 'that he read them often, and kept a set in every one of his residences; that he himself had thought it right to inform His Royal Highness that Miss Austen was staying in London'.

This was probably the first recognition and acknowledgement as an author, outside of her family circle, that Jane Austen had received and one of few during her lifetime. Her nephew James Austen-Leigh confirmed that it was 'the only mark of distinction ever bestowed upon her'.

The equestrian statue of King George IV (former Prince Regent), Trafalgar Square, London. (Author's collection)

The Prince Regent was told that Jane was currently residing in London, but despite admiring her work, he did not request to meet her in person. Instead, he asked the Reverend James Stanier Clarke, the royal librarian, to show her around the library and Carlton House, his London residence which overlooked Pall Mall and St James's Park. During that visit on 13 November 1815, Clarke intimated that if Jane had any forthcoming publications, she was invited to dedicate that work to the Prince Regent.

This placed Jane in a dilemma because she did not regard the Prince Regent favourably because of his decadent lifestyle which was incompatible with the values of love, friendship and family, together with good manners, that she advocated in her novels. She had frowned upon the Prince Regent's treatment of his wife, Princess Caroline. 'Poor woman,' Jane wrote, 'I shall support her as long as I can, because she is a woman and because I hate her husband.'

Despite her personal feelings, Jane was persuaded by John Murray that by royal command she must dedicate *Emma* to the Prince Regent. Before the publication date, Jane sent the Reverend Clarke a letter on 11 December 1815 advising him that she had arranged for a specially bound edition of the three-volume set featuring the Prince of Wales feathers on the spine to be printed for the Prince Regent.

46. Jane Austen's Donkey Carriage

Used by Jane Austen during her illness

Location: Jane Austen's House, Winchester Road, Chawton, GU34 1BA

Map co-ordinates: 51°07′58.9″N 0°59′20.0″W; decimal: 51.133037, -0.988899

It is thought that this donkey cart was made for the Austen women when they arrived at Chawton in 1809. Jane was an avid walker, but this donkey cart gave her greater mobility and she used it to visit friends and as a quick means of travel to the shops in Alton. Although in the wintertime she would be exposed to the wind and rain, using this cart would prevent her shoes and dress from getting dirty on the muddy country lanes. Sometimes bad weather meant that trips had to be abandoned. On 9 July 1816, Jane wrote:

> Mary Jane and I have been wet through once already today, we set off in the Donkey Carriage for Farringdon as I wanted to see the improvements Mr Woolls is making, but we were obliged to turn back before we got there, but not too soon enough to avoid a pelter all the way home.

The Austens would have kept two donkeys, and they grazed in the orchard. It was an affordable means to travel in and around the Chawton area. Although most of Jane's characters travelled by horse or carriages, Mrs Elton in *Emma* acknowledges the benefits for women of keeping donkeys, including allowing them to get out of the house:

Jane Austen's donkey carriage. (Author's collection)

> I wish we had a donkey. The thing would be for us all to come on donkeys, Jane, Miss Bates, and me – and my *caro sposo* walking by. I really must talk to him about purchasing a donkey. In a country life I conceive it to be a sort of necessary; for, let a woman have ever so many resources, it is not possible for her to be always shut up at home; – and very long walks, you know – in summer there is dust, and in winter there is dirt.

As her health began to decline during 1816, Jane became weak and was unable to go for long walks. To enjoy the fresh air, she would have been reliant on the donkey carriage to transport her around Chawton. However, as the winter approached it was too cold to use the donkey carriage and, on 24 January 1817, she wrote that 'this is not the time of year for donkey-carriages, and our donkeys are necessarily having so long a run of luxurious idleness that I suppose we shall find they have forgotten much of their education when we use them again'.

Jane used the donkey carriage on 26 March 1817 as she confirmed this in a letter to her niece Caroline: 'I have taken one ride on the donkey and like it very much.' Jane had hoped that she would regain her strength by the summer of 1817 and be strong enough to walk into Alton and not need to use the donkey carriage, but that was not to be.

47. No. 4 High Street, Alton, Hampshire

Home of Jane Austen's doctor

Location: No. 4 High Street, Alton, GU34 1BA

Map co-ordinates: 51°08′59.8″N 0°58′26.0″W; decimal: 51.149932, -0.973883

Dr William Curtis, Jane Austen's surgeon apothecary, whom she called her 'Alton Apothy', lived in this house. On 13 June 1814, Jane refers to Miss Benn, her neighbour who lived at Thatch Cottage in Chawton, visiting Dr Curtis regarding her hand.

On 6 April 1817, Jane told her brother Charles that she was seen by Dr Curtis and that she was feeling better. However, by May 1817, her health had deteriorated. Dr Curtis advised Jane that he had done all he could and that she should seek treatment elsewhere. This was an ominous situation and despite not being able to cure Jane, he recommended that she go to Winchester to see Dr Giles King Lyford, who was highly regarded by London practitioners. Jane agreed to Dr Curtis's recommendation and she departed from Chawton Cottage for the last time on 24 May 1817.

Above and right: No. 4 High Street, home of Dr William Curtis, and the plaque commemorating his association with Jane Austen. (Author's collection)

48. No. 8 College Street, Winchester

Jane Austen spent the final eight weeks of her life here

Location: No. 8 College Street, Winchester, SO23 9LX

Map co-ordinates: 51°03′31.4″N 1°18′49.2″W; decimal: 51.058725, -1.313671

Jane sought medical advice from Dr Giles King Lyford, a physician who practised at the County Hospital in Winchester. She lodged in No. 8 College Street from 24 May 1817. Three days later she wrote favourably of her accommodation: 'Our lodgings are very comfortable. We have a neat little drawing room with a bow window overlooking Dr. Gabell's garden.'

The bow window that Jane was referring to was at the front of the house on the first floor. Cassandra would care for her sister in the drawing room. Jane was confined to the sofa and on one occasion was taken outside into Winchester in a sedan chair. Jane hoped to venture outside again in a wheelchair but her deteriorating health prevented her from doing that.

Two days before her death she wrote some verses to a satirical poem entitled 'Venta' which was about the Winchester Races being held on St Swithin's Day. During the early hours of the morning on 18 July 1817, Jane Austen died in the drawing room of No. 8 College Street. Cassandra recalled her final moments:

> She felt herself to be dying about half-an-hour before she became tranquil and apparently unconscious. During that half-hour was her struggle poor soul! She said she could not tell us

Jane Austen spent the last eight weeks of her life in this house at No. 8 College Street, Winchester. (Author's collection)

The plaque commemorating Jane Austen's final home. (Author's collection)

> what she suffered, though she complained of little fixed pain. When I asked her if there was anything she wanted, her answer was she wanted nothing but death, and some of her words were: 'God grant me patience, pray for me, oh pray for me!'

Although Jane's cause of death was unclear, some modern doctors have suggested that either Addison's disease, Hodgkin's lymphoma (a type of blood cancer), or Bovine TB could have been responsible for her premature death at the age of forty-one.

On 24 July 1817, it was from No. 8 College Street that Jane Austen's coffin was taken for burial in Winchester Cathedral. Cassandra stood outside the house and watched as her funeral cortège proceeded along College Street and turned right into the precincts of the cathedral. Cassandra wrote, 'I watched the little mournful procession the length of the street; and when it turned from my sight, and I had lost her forever … Never was human being more sincerely mourned by those who attended her remains as this poor creature.'

49. Jane Austen's Tomb, Winchester Cathedral

Her final resting place

Location: Winchester Cathedral, The Close, Winchester, SO23 9LS

Map co-ordinates: 51°03′39.5″N 1°18′52.6″W; decimal: 51.060980, -1.314598

Winchester Cathedral was constructed between 1079 and 1532 and is renowned as the burial place of Jane Austen. It is not known why Jane was buried here instead of St Nicholas Church, Chawton, which was only 16 miles away and would have been a suitable resting place close to her home and family. Furthermore, she did not have any direct connections with Winchester and was an unknown author to the public. It is surmised that her brother Henry decided upon this location as his sister's final resting place because he knew the Bishop of Winchester and he may have told him that the Prince Regent admired her work.

Above left: Jane Austen's tomb in the north aisle of Winchester Cathedral. (Author's collection)

Above right: The memorial dedicated to Jane Austen, situated in the north aisle of Winchester Cathedral, close to her grave. (Author's collection)

Winchester Cathedral. (Author's collection)

Jane made her appreciation of the cathedral known to her family and that may have also been taken into consideration when deciding on where she should be interred.

Before the funeral, Cassandra Austen lamented, 'The last sad ceremony is to take place on Thursday morning; her dear remains are to be deposited in the Cathedral. It is a satisfaction to me to think that they are to lie in a building she admired so much.'

On 24 July 1817, Jane Austen's funeral cortège arrived at Winchester Cathedral. It was an early funeral service and burial had to be completed before the morning service, which was scheduled for 10 a.m. Jane was buried in the north aisle. The epitaph inscribed on her black marble tombstone was written by her brother James. Given that she was virtually unknown at the time of her death, James focused upon her attributes as a person and faith, 'the benevolence of her heart, the sweetness of her temper, and the extraordinary endowments of her mind'. However, he omitted to mention that Jane was an author.

Public interest in Jane was aroused in 1870 when her nephew James Austen-Leigh published a memoir of his authoress aunt. During that same year he arranged for a brass plaque detailing her literary accomplishments to be fixed on the wall close to her grave.

50. Jane Austen Memorial, Westminster Abbey

Jane Austen commemorated in Poets' Corner

Location: Westminster Abbey, 20 Dean's Yard, London, SW1P 3PA

Map co-ordinates: 51°29′58.3″N 0°07′44.0″W; decimal: 51.499518, -0.128887

Poets' Corner, in the south transept of Westminster Abbey, is where British literary figures are either buried or commemorated with a memorial. Geoffrey Chaucer was the first poet interred here in 1400 and during successive centuries the nation's literary giants followed. Jane Austen was commemorated with a tablet at Poets' Corner 150 years after her death.

During her lifetime, Jane never mixed in literary circles and was not widely known. It wasn't until after her death that her work was recognised and it is appropriate that her name is remembered alongside other eminent British writers in Poets' Corner such as William Shakespeare, Charles Dickens, Thomas Hardy and the Brontë sisters. Her brother Henry wrote, 'Her reading was very extensive in history and belles-lettres and her memory extremely tenacious. Her favourite moral writers were Johnson in prose and Cowper in verse.'

The tablet commemorating Jane Austen in Poets' Corner. (Copyright: Dean and Chapter of Westminster)

Westminster Abbey. (Author's collection)

A small tablet dedicated to Jane Austen was unveiled on 17 December 1967. The tablet, made from polished Roman stone, was donated by the Jane Austen Society. It was placed next to Shakespeare's memorial and beneath the memorial to Dr Samuel Johnson, an author whom she admired. Above Johnson is the bust of Robert Southey, one of her peers who admired her work. The tablet also overlooks the graves of Charles Dickens and Thomas Hardy.

Bibliography

Austen, Caroline, *Reminiscences of Caroline Austen* (Jane Austen Society, 1986)

Austen-Leigh, James Edward, *A Memoir of Jane Austen* (Richard Bentley & Son, London 1879)

Austen-Leigh, Mary Augusta, *Personal Aspects of Jane Austen* (John Murray, London, 1920)

Austen-Leigh, Richard and William, *Jane Austen Her Life & Letters, A Family Record* (E. P. Dutton & Co., New York, 1913)

Brabourne, Edward Lord, *Letters of Jane Austen, Volumes 1 & 2* (Richard Bentley & Son, London, 1884)

Egan, Pierce, *Walks through Bath* (Meyler and Son, London, 1819)

Feltham, John, *A Guide to all the watering places* (R. Philips, London, 1806)

Hubback, Edith and J. H., *Jane Austen's Sailor Brothers* (John Lane Company, New York, 1906)

Laski, Marghanita, *Jane Austen and her World* (Thames & Hudson, London, 1969)

Le Faye, Deirdre, *Jane Austen, A Family Record* (The British Library, 1989)